DO PEOPLE GROW ON
FAMILY TREES?

DO PEOPLE GROW ON FAMILY TREES?

Genealogy for Kids & Other Beginners

ELLIS ISLAND
1892–1992

THE OFFICIAL ELLIS ISLAND HANDBOOK

•

BY IRA WOLFMAN

•

Foreword by Alex Haley

•

Illustrations by Michael Klein

WORKMAN PUBLISHING, NEW YORK

This book is dedicated to the millions of brave people
who left home to begin anew—and especially to the
memory of my own immigrant ancestors, Ida Fudelowicz
and Morris Wolfman, Edna Burstein and Hymen Perlo.

■

Library of Congress Cataloging-in-Publication Data

Wolfman, Ira.

Do People Grow on Family Trees? Genealogy for Kids and Other Beginners

p. cm.

Summary: A guide to finding out one's own family history and how to formally record it.

ISBN 0-89480-348-4

1. Genealogy—Juvenile literature. [1. Genealogy.] I. Title.

CS15.5.W65 1990

929'.1—dc20   88-51586

CIP

AC

Book design by Mark Freiman and Tom Starace

Cover illustration by Reynold Ruffins

Workman Publishing Company, Inc.

708 Broadway

New York, New York 10003

Manufactured in the United States of America

10 9 8 7 6 5 4 3 2

Thank You

This book could not have been written without a great deal of support and assistance. My deepest thanks to all who offered advice and aid, including:

Alex Haley, for his great generosity and support; the Statue of Liberty/Ellis Island Foundation, especially Barbara Graziano, Peg Zitko, and Ziva Benderly; Barbara Cohen of Manhattan's fabulous New York Bound Bookshop, for resources, ideas, and help; Johni Cerni of Lineages, who kindly shared her family tales; Elsdon Smith, America's dean of names; Dolores Healy and the many other helpful people at the Balch Institute; Miriam Weiner for sharing her genealogical expertise and her fine photo collection; Eileen Polakoff for her advice, counsel, and all-around, much-appreciated help; The Jewish Genealogical Society, with special thanks to Michael Brenner, Gary Mokotoff, Steven W. Siegel, and Rabbi Malcolm Stern for his "Ten Commandments"; Sharlott Blevins of the Federation of Genealogical Soci-

eties; Madeline Franco at Ancestry; Steve Turner of the National Writers Union and Alvin Mass, both of whom offered important help to a writer in distress; Marshall Beil and Kate Dodge, who graciously smoothed my way; Mel Hanberg, who helped me rediscover some of my missing links; David and Lilia Seegmiller and the New York City LDS Family History Library, who aided me in my search for those links; Louise Gikow and Ellen Weiss, my publishing links; The Wertheim Study at the New York Public Library; Dan Rolph of Philadelphia Historical Society; Ina Stern, my ombudsperson; The Galloway, Kauaua, Spencer, and many other families who let me peek at their trees; Charlotte Waggoner, for sharing her Wares; Allen Sheinman, for eagerly supporting the research; Jackie Leo, Nancy Clark, and Susan Ungaro at *Family Circle,* and Harriet Lyons at the *Daily News,* for editorial enthusiasm above the call of duty; Julia, who came with me to Ellis the very first time I set foot on that special island, and who encouraged my writing about it; Linc

and Joan, for their generosity and faith in me; Nora and Rolf, for fanning the spark that was my interest in Ellis Island; Sally Kovalchick, for her good cheer, editorial guidance, and openness to change on our long road to publication; Mary Wilkinson, for her fine editorial polishing; Rona Beame, for her enthusiastic and excellent work gathering illustrations; Tom Starace, for putting it all together; Julie Hansen, for her willingness to help; my closest ancestors, Mom and Dad, for old photographs, new memories, good humor, and loads of patience; my sister Sharon, brother-in-law Ilan, and nieces Lauren and Keren Zarom; my newly re-discovered cousin Harvey Burstein; my late, wonderful, spunky great-aunt Tanta Blima; Hyman Small, an inspiration and a piece of living history at 102 years old; Evan, for being his wondrous self and for wondering when I would finish "his" book; Ronda, for enduring all and sticking with me through thin, thick, and thickheadedness; and the many other friends and genealogists who shared my excitement and helped me along the way.

Foreword

By Alex Haley

How I wish I could have read this book when I was a child. If I had, I would have been so much more aware that my grandparents were a source of riches beyond belief. I would have known that the stories they told—stories about themselves, their parents, and their grandparents—were gifts more precious than the greatest of treasures.

If I'd been aware of these things as a child, I would have known to listen much more closely to my family, and to keep a notebook of what they said. I would have known what further questions to ask—questions seeking anything and everything they knew about our history.

And I know they would have loved telling me.

Because both of my parents were teachers, they saw to it that most of my presents were books. It tingles me today to think that if I had been given this book, I would have plied my elders about every aspect of their lives. Where did they live? What work did they do? What clothing did they wear? What games did they play as children? Tell me, I could have asked, what was it like when your family went to church?

I could have kept notebooks from early on. I could have sketched and written descriptions of what my elders told me about how they dressed, or their games, or the horses and mules and wagons and buggies that were their transportation. And of the cotton and tobacco farms where they worked.

It strikes me as significant that two of the most popular books of modern times were written by authors who had once been grandchildren in Southern families, sitting and listening as their elders frequently, proudly, told family stories.

One of these grandchildren was a little girl from Atlanta, Georgia, whose name was Margaret Mitchell. For years, Margaret heard the family stories, and was taken as a child to visit Civil War sites on the outskirts of Atlanta. She would grow up to write a book that, along with its later motion picture, would fascinate the whole world. The book and the film were, of course, *Gone With the Wind*.

The second book was my own *Roots*, which was born on the front porch of a gray-frame home in the very small town of Henning, Tennessee. After the death of my grandfather the year that I was five, my deeply grieving Grandma Cynthia Palmer wrote asking her five sisters to come and visit the next summer. And they all did.

A pattern quickly developed: After supper in the evenings, they would gather on the front porch in their rocking chairs. Dipping snuff, which they skeeted out over the honeysuckle vines and the blinking fireflies, they talked night after night about their own childhoods as the children of former slave parents Tom and Irene Murray. Their daddy was a strong, stern blacksmith. And they talked most of all about his daddy, their grandfather, my great-grandfather, a most colorful slave gamecock fighter whose name was George Lea, and whom everybody called by his nickname of "Chicken George."

They recalled his mother, who lived in Spotsylvania County, Virginia, and was called Miss Kizzy. And then her parents—the Big House cook Miss Bell and the master's buggy driver, an African, who said that his African name was Kinte.

I sat listening night after night, until the ancestral family stories became fixed in my memory. It would be 40 years later that I would remember and decide to try to research the skeletal story I'd heard. The eventual result was the book and its television mini-series, *Roots*.

And now I'm astonished to think how much more I could have learned from those dear ladies on the front porch if only I'd known to ask them questions, as I would have—if only I had read this book.

Contents

Chapter One: Where You Came From

Chapter Two: How We Got Here

Chapter Three: Finding Your Families

Chapter Four: Coming to America

Chapter Five: Exploring the Past

Chapter Six: Becoming an American

Chapter Seven: The Name Game

Chapter Eight: The Paper Chase

Chapter Nine: You Could Look It Up

Chapter Ten: Sharing the Wealth

How to Help Others Enjoy Your Genealogical Discoveries.

Appendix

Index

How I Became an Ancestor Detector

It was a hot summer day in Washington, D.C., but I hardly noticed. While other people were working or touring or going to the beach, I was on a manhunt.

I was looking for my grandfather.

I was in a library in a majestic building called "The National Archives of the United States of America," where historic American documents and records are kept. In front of me was a list of people who had come to America by ship in the early 1900s. These lists, called "passenger lists" or "ship's manifests," were part of the curious mystery I was examining.

I'd recently learned that three men—all of them with exactly the same name as my father's father—had entered the United States between 1900 and 1910. They were born in different years, so I was sure that only one could be *my* grandfather. But which one?

I was determined to find out.

The men had arrived on three different ships. I found the passenger list of the first ship, the S.S. *Belgravia*. It had left Hamburg, Germany, for New York City on December 12, 1902, with more than 1,350 people on board. The list was gigantic: 45 pages long, with 30 names on each page. And every name was written in the same cramped, hard-to-read handwriting.

I took a deep breath, then started on page one. Around me, other people appeared to be working hard on their own mysteries.

After about an hour, I came to page 30, line 30. And then, even though I was in a library, I yelled.

There he was! I was sure this was *my* grandfather because the manifest named the tiny town—Lapiz, Russia—from which I knew he had come.

I can't explain exactly what made seeing my grandfather's name so moving. But finding him in that long list thrilled me. I read every bit of information the manifest had about him. He was barely 21 years old, single, and could read and write. His trade was listed as "tailor," his nationality as "Hebrew." He was to stay with an uncle in Brooklyn. And he had $3 with him.

I'd known my grandfather as a kind old man who moved slowly and spoke English softly, with an accent. But until this moment, I'd never thought of him as a courageous boy who—by himself!—had taken a giant ship and traveled thousands of miles in the middle of winter to move forever to a new country whose language he didn't

Morris and Ida Wolfman and their son Ben, around 1916. On line 30 of the boat manifest, note Morris's name (Moische Wolfmann).

even speak.

I wanted to hold on to this bit of family history. I made copies of the page and took them with me. When I shared them with my parents, they were as excited as I had been.

This day at the National Archives was one of my first experiences as an "Ancestor Detector." That's my term for people who track down clues about their own long-ago relatives—their ancestors.

Over the next few years, I did a lot of detecting. I found out when my other grandparents arrived in America. I interviewed relatives and heard stories about their lives. I learned a lot about the little towns in Europe that my grandparents had once called home. I uncovered all kinds of records and documents about my relatives' past. I also discovered the names of relatives who had long been forgotten—including those of my *great-great-great-great* grandparents, who were born in the 1750s!

As time went on, my hobby became more and more exciting. I was learning so much—I was exploring my own family's history, about which I'd known so little. I wasn't just finding relatives. In a way, I felt I was saving their lives, bringing them back to memory.

When I shared my discoveries with people, they started thinking about their own families. Soon, my friends were interested in researching *their* backgrounds.

While I thought of myself as an Ancestor Detector, anyone looking at what I was doing would have said, "Oh, you're interested in genealogy." And they would have been right.

Genealogy is the record of a family's history. Every family, no matter where it comes from, has its own long and fascinating story. That's true whether your family has lived in the United States for two years or two hundred.

Exploring your family's history can be an adventure. You may uncover heroic tales of a dashing ancestor's life, or the ancient legends of a town where

At Morris and Ida's home, around 1955.

your family lived for hundreds of years.

But genealogy isn't just about ancestors. It's also about *you*. You are a part of history—and you've already left many clues about yourself for the future.

This book shows you how that's true. It will help you find out how you've been influenced by people you never knew. You'll learn how to write your own life story, and organize the story of your ancestors' lives. You'll discover how nicknames became last names, and what your own name may say about your family. You'll poke into the history of your family's arrival in your hometown, city, or state. You'll hear the amazing story of immigration to this country, then look for your family's place in that story.

The best part of genealogy is that it helps people discover their own specialness. Your ancestors are a part of the history of the world. Your family has played a part in the building of the United States. Whether your family is large or small, traditional "mom-and-dad" or sprawling step-family, you have a proud heritage and a history that is all your own.

CHAPTER ONE

Where You Came From

A LOOK INTO YOUR PAST

Have you ever thought of your life as a mystery? It is, in many ways.

Your future is certainly filled with mystery: what you are going to do with your life; where you will live; who will become part of your family. The only way to solve the mystery of your future is to live it.

Your past is a mystery, too. Where did you come from? How did you end up *where* you are—and *who* you are? Who were your ancestors, the people who came before you?

Obviously, you already know that you were born to two parents. You probably know your grandparents, and

In 1908, this Dutch immigrant mother and her 11 children lined up at Ellis Island for a photograph before taking a train to their new home in Minnesota. The kids look as if they are wearing their best clothing for the long trip.

you may have heard many stories about their lives.

But how far back can you go into your family's past? Can you name any of your grandparents' parents? Do you know where they came from? Do you have any idea what they looked like and what their lives were like?

"Well," you might say, "what difference does it make who my great-grandfather was? Who really cares?"

You should—because you are the descendant of people who were alive hundreds of years ago, and each of the relatives who came before you has played a critical role in determining who you are. If *any one* of your ancestors had lived his or her life differently, everyone who came after that person would have been very different. If your ancestors had not had the courage to change their lives, to move, to risk, you would not be where or who you are today.

You are the latest chapter, the newest news, in a remarkable line of people and history. Which parent do you most resemble? Do you have blond hair or brown eyes? Do you notice any habits or likes and dislikes that you have in common with other members of your family? At least some of these traits are inherited—part of your heritage, your connection to your ancestors.

Everyone on earth has a long and colorful history, with a wide variety of ancestors. Most people, however, haven't given much thought to them. Some people never dreamed their relatives had a past worth knowing about. Others doubted that they could ever track down their "genealogy"—the record of their ancestral background.

In fact, you *can* rediscover your ancestors. With some detective work, you may find out their names, and where and when they lived. But there's much more to genealogy than just writing down names and dates. Genealogy is also a story—the story of a family, of their place in history.

What were your ancestors' lives like? How did the great events of their time affect them? What was important to them? What made them do the things they did? These are long-lost mysteries for most families, details of lives now forgotten, but you may be able to uncover the answers. All you need is time, the desire to learn more, and a bit of historical background.

How do you begin? There is a simple rule that all genealogists follow: Start with what you know; begin with the present, and use what you know to take you to what you don't know.

Using this rule, you will be able to uncover many surprising things. Looking at your own life will lead you to facts about your parents' lives. Finding out about their history will give you clues that may lead you to your grandparents' stories. And their stories may lead you to other ancestors.

What will you have when you are finished? A huge collection of family names, stories, recipes, photographs, special possessions, and news. With a little bit of work, you will find copies of documents from the past. With a little

Kids at Ellis Island: Above, Scottish children dressed in traditional costumes. At right, two Italian children in 1905.

A Hungarian immigrant and her four daughters. Women and children under 16 could not leave Ellis Island alone; someone already in America had to vouch for them.

bit of luck, you will learn about family who lived 100—or even 200 years ago. You may be able to track down papers that showed when your ancestors became citizens of the United States or find their names on the actual passenger list of the boat that brought them here.

You can put all of this material together in a loose-leaf notebook and share it with your friends and family today. Even better, the record of your family's history can be a present from you to the people in *your* future.

You may be thinking, "I'll never be able to do all this. It sounds very complicated." Once you begin, however, you'll see how exciting genealogy is.

Here are three short stories of people who made amazing discoveries in their genealogical hunts.

A Very Big Bedtime Story

As a young girl, Charlotte Littlejohn noticed something odd when she visited her grandmother, Almeda Elizabeth Ware Fenley, in Texas. "My grandmother was a short woman, but all her brothers were very tall," Charlotte recalls today. "I was intrigued by the tallest ones, Uncle Oscar and Uncle Ira. They were six feet nine and seven feet tall!

"When I asked my grandmother about them, she told me that somewhere in England there was a giant bed built especially for one of her ancestors."

Grandma Almeda had been told about the bed by *her* father, J.C. Ware. He said it was built around 1600, and that it was gigantic—about nine feet long. Her father claimed the bed had to be put together in the room where it was to be used because no one wanted to think about moving it.

The Great Bed of Ware.

"My grandma had no dates for what happened afterward," Charlotte notes, "but she said she'd heard that the man who had the bed made moved to Ireland and couldn't take it with him."

Grandma wasn't sure whether the bed still existed.

This story stayed in Charlotte's mind. Years later she met with Eileen Mundy, a cousin who had just returned from studying the family history in England. Eileen told Charlotte, "That bed exists. I found a notation about it in a book—it's known as 'The Great Bed of Ware'—and I've been told it's still in England somewhere. I just don't know where."

Then Charlotte and her husband, Jack Waggoner, took a trip to England. One day they were looking at a map and noticed a little town outside London named Ware. "Let's go see," Charlotte said. They drove to Ware and walked around town, asking if anyone knew about a huge bed. It wasn't until they met an elderly man in a pub that they got their answer. "Oh yes, that was here for a long while. They kept it in an inn, but it's gone now. It's at the Victoria and Albert Museum in London."

The couple rushed back to London, and Charlotte made a beeline for the museum. She asked a guard for directions, and he brought her to a corner of the museum. There it was: The Great Bed of Ware, a nine-foot-long by nine-foot-wide bed with a huge wooden canopy, made before 1600.

Charlotte stared and stared. "I had this wonderful feeling that there was a basis to my family stories."

She had only one regret: "I just wish my grandma had been there to see it, too."

Your many families

When we talk about tracing your family history, it sounds as if you have only *one* family. But that's not true. You actually have many families.

You start, of course, with your immediate family—your parents and yourself. But very soon you'll be thinking about your four grandparents—each of whom came from a different family. Your research, therefore, will include your mom's mother's family and your mom's father's family, and your dad's father's family and your dad's mother's family.

How can you research so many families? The answer is, you can't. As you dig deeper into the past, you will find that one branch of your family is easier to trace than the others. That's the one you will work on most. (But of course, if at any time you come across clues about another branch, you should follow the trail as far as you can.)

Remember that one of the nice things about genealogy is that it is a lifetime hobby, so just research those families of yours one at a time.

Alex Haley, author of Roots.

An Unexpected Route to History

"I'd always heard my grandma tell stories about our ancestors," the 60-year-old man said. "Then one Saturday afternoon, I was in Washington, D.C., poking along on the sidewalk of the Mall. I looked up and saw a big building with the words 'Archives of the United States' written across its front.

"I wandered in without any specific reason. Someone startled me by asking, 'Can I help you?' I heard myself say, 'I wonder if I could see the 1870 census records for Alamance County, North Carolina.'

"I went to the microfilm room, put the census on the reader, and turned and turned the handle. I was fascinated. Here were all these names of people long gone, and descriptions of their families. I felt as if I were standing on the side of the road, watching them.

"And then I found something that astonished me: the name of my grandma's daddy, Thomas Murray. How many times had I heard grandma talk about him? And there he was, her daddy, a blacksmith. His wife. Their children.

"That was my first bite of the genealogical bug, from which there is no cure."

This story was told by journalist Alex Haley. When he began this trip into his genealogy in the 1960s, he didn't quite know what he was looking for or where it would lead. Haley had spent many nights listening to his grandma tell stories about his ancestors. He knew his family had been in America for nearly 200 years, and he had heard ancestors' names and the names of a few places, like 'Naplis and Alamance County.

"When I walked into the archives, the idea of writing a book was as far away from me as the Man in the Moon," Haley recalled. But when he found his great-grandfather's name on official records in Washington, D.C., it changed him. Soon, he began to work on a book about his family.

Nine years later—after thousands of hours of research and trips across the United States, to England, and to Africa—*Roots*, Haley's book about his

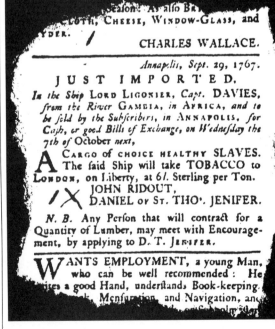

This 1767 newspaper ad announced the arrival of a slave ship. Alex Haley's ancestor was aboard.

On a visit to Africa, Alex Haley met his sixth cousins. All the people in this photo are descended from the same great-great-great-great-great-grandparent.

At left, this ancestor of Alex Haley was known as Chicken George; born a slave, he died a free man. At right, Alex and his brother, George Haley, talk family history with "cousin" Georgia Henderson.

family, was published.

Roots tells, in dramatic fashion, the story of Kunta, a young African boy who was kidnapped and brought to the English colonies in America in September of 1767. The book traces the painful and courageous lives of Kunta's descendants through slavery, the Civil War, emancipation, and the world wars. It follows the descendants right up to the 1970s. One of those descendants was, of course, Alex Haley.

Haley's story startled America. A descendant of slaves could find his own ancestors? How was that possible? Wasn't genealogy only for rich people, for aristocrats?

Haley proved that even a descendant of poor people could find and tell his own distinguished and important story. *Roots* became a bestseller and one of the most popular TV shows ever broadcast.

"All human beings belong to some family that has ancestry and a native land," Haley now says. "The need for knowing who you are is universal.

"I've traveled around the world since *Roots* came out. Everywhere I speak—Egypt, Mexico, Peking, Paris—people come up to me with their family charts. Everyone can gain something—something that is immense—by knowing where they came from."

A Phone Call to the Past

One day, 15 years ago, the telephone rang in Joan Lince's home. By answering it, she changed her life.

"It was a man on the West Coast I'd never met. He said he'd found my name in a phone directory, and wondered, because we spelled our last names the same way, if we were related."

It turned out that they weren't, but her caller was able to put Joan in touch with people in Oregon he thought might be her relatives. The next week she called them—and over a speakerphone, had a conversation with five strangers who turned into family.

"These were people I'd never known, but they knew all about me. 'Oh, yes,' one woman said, 'you went to college in Michigan.' We must have talked for an hour. When I hung up, I thought, 'How wonderful to have recovered lost members of my family.' "

From that day on, Joan Lince was hooked. She has traced her family history back to the early 1600s, recovered a long-lost journal kept by her great-great-grandfather—and had a

Joan Lince's great-great-grandfather, John Husted, lived from 1795 to 1890.

wonderful time doing it. "Genealogy is so much fun," she says. "You find leads and then you find more; you learn skills and then you can do so much more."

Your search may not lead you to find an artifact, or write a book, or discover a long-lost branch of your family. But it will put you in touch with the people you came from and it will make their past come alive. "The relatives I never knew were just names to me," geneal-

Buddy, can you spare an ancestor?

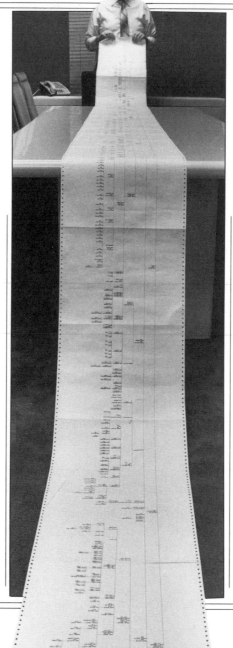

Gary Mokotoff unrolls his 30-foot-long family tree, which he compiled on a computer.

How many ancestors do you think you have? If you start with your parents, then count their parents, and their parents' parents, how many people are there? And what if you go a few steps beyond that?

Each level of your family is called a "generation." Go back one generation and you find your parents. Look back two, and there are your grandparents. When you look back three generations, you reach your grandparents' parents—your great-grandparents.

A chart showing only your parents, grandparents, and great-grandparents would include fourteen people (two parents, four grandparents, and eight great-grandparents).

But each of your eight great-grandparents had two parents, and each of those sixteen great-great-grandparents had two parents. By the time of your great-great-great-great-grandparents (what genealogists call your "fourth great-grandparents"), there would be 126 people on the chart. And if you went back three more generations, your chart would have over 1,000 people on it!

If you were able to go back twenty generations, you'd arrive somewhere before the year 1400. In that time, you might find yourself with over two million direct ancestors!

Actually, however, genealogists estimate that the number of *different* people on your family tree would more likely be only about *one* million, because so many distant cousins married each other without being aware that they were related.

That's still a pretty big group for a family reunion!

ogist Miriam Weiner remembers. "But then I researched them. What I've learned made me admire them so much. It reconnected me to who I am."

Great personal discoveries also await you. As you trace your own family's path, you will see how it fits into the larger picture. You will read about the great tale of immigration to this part of the world, and come to understand the struggles and courage of people who yearned to be Americans.

Finding all this information takes time, however. Your family's history is a huge jigsaw puzzle. The pieces are your ancestors' names and the details of their lives, and they are scattered all over the world.

If you were living in another country, that might not be true. In most of the world, a family's history may extend back hundreds and hundreds of years in one place. But the United States is not like those countries. Just about everyone in this country has roots that reach back to somewhere else.

In order to really understand your own family's history, you will have to look at the story of how *everyone* got here—the great tale of American immigration.

Out for a bike ride in 1899 was Joan Lince's father's mother, Alta Belle Conklin (right), and a friend.

Joan Lince and her cousin Ray, around 1990.

CHAPTER TWO

How We Got Here

THE STORY OF AMERICAN IMMIGRATION

Try as she might, 13-year-old Maryashe could not fall asleep. Her mind was buzzing, thinking about how her life was about to change.

"Excitement kept me awake. . . . In the morning I was going away from Polotzk, forever and ever. I was going on a wonderful journey. . . to America. How could I sleep? . . . A million suns shone out for every star. The winds rushed in from outer space, roaring in my ears, 'America! America!' "

What could be more thrilling than imagining a new life in the United States of America, that magical land across the sea? No wonder Maryashe, living in the little Russian village of

Polotzk in the 1890s, was so excited.

Millions of people—young and old—had the same reaction. Since the 1600s, the land we call the United States has been a magnet to the rest of the world. Over the last 200 years, nearly 50 *million* people from 140 countries have left their homelands to live here. That has been the greatest movement of people from one place to another in world history.

They came from cold northern European countries and tropical Caribbean islands, from faraway China and Korea and nearby Mexico and Canada. They came in sailing ships, on buses, on jet planes, and on foot. Some arrived hundreds of years ago. Some arrived a generation ago. And some arrived last week.

Someone in your family was probably among them. Almost every American is descended from ancestors who came here from another country. For most people, the trip to America was both exciting and frightening. They had to leave behind their friends and family and endure great hardships to come to a wild and untamed land where the culture was different and the language strange. They risked whatever little they had to begin anew because they believed in a dream

Escaping to freedom: On a November day in 1956, this Hungarian family crossed the border to Austria, escaping the Russian crackdown in their homeland.

called America.

The dream was of a country where life was better, where there was land for all people who wanted it, where no one went hungry and jobs and opportunities were plentiful. In that dream nation, people could speak and pray as they wished, without fear.

This vision was appealing to so many people for one reason: It was completely different from the lives they were living.

In many countries, people lived in terrible poverty. In the countryside, small farmers struggled mightily just to feed their families. Men and women worked from dawn till dusk. Families had no luxuries and little free time. Few children could go to school—they had to help with the family's work. Most poor people could not read, or even write their own names.

Worst of all, they had little reason to believe life would ever get better.

"We were serfs bound to a heartless master who cared nothing about us," Russian-born Boris Treschoff remembered his father telling him. "We worked hard and received nothing except the bare necessities. . . . We had been peasants, living on the same plot of land for generations. My ancestors were born, lived, worked, and died

A thatched-roof stone cottage in the Old Country. Several families lived together in this house in Ireland in the 1880s. One of the great challenges of your genealogical hunt will be to find out more about your ancestors' lives. What kind of homes did they live in?

there. They did not dare to think about going to any other place. Where would they go without finding life the same? No, there was no hope anywhere."

In China, too, life was a terrible struggle. "My mother still talks of the poverty in Fragrant Mountains [a village in Canton province]," writer Jade Snow Wong recalled. "If they had rice, they were fortunate. If there was salt or oil, they were even more fortunate.

Meat and fish were rarities."

The details differ from country to country, but everywhere there was a similar hopelessness:
● In Norway, the land was rocky and little grew easily. Small farmers could barely harvest enough food to feed their own families.
● In Italy, rich landowners leased poor farmers a tiny plot of land to plant—and then demanded part of the crop as

payment.
● In the German-speaking areas of Europe, millions of farmers tended small farms. When their crops failed in the 1840s, many could not support their families.

A few years later, a German political movement for democracy was smashed. Thousands of people who had spoken out were no longer welcome in their homeland.

Comings and goings

Two words that are sometimes confused are "emigrant" and "immigrant." They mean different things, but they have a lot in common: Every emigrant is also an immigrant.

To *migrate* means "to move from one place to another." The prefix *em* means "away from." The prefix *im* means "going into." *Emigrants* leave their country to live somewhere else permanently. *Immigrants* arrive from another land, hoping to make their home permanently in their new country.

When you hear people called emigrants, that refers to where they came from. And when you hear talk about immigrants, that refers to where they went.

Min Jae's family left Korea to resettle in the United States. They emigrated from Korea, and immigrated to America. To the Korean government, they were emigrants. To the American government, they were immigrants.

● In Ireland, life went from difficult to terrible. England had sent soldiers to occupy the island. They were hated by many Irish, who fought to be free of English rule. Then in the mid-1840s, disaster struck. More than a million died during "The Great Potato Famine" because the potato crop—which poor people depended upon for food—had been destroyed by disease.

● For Jews across eastern Europe, poverty and prejudice were part of everyday life. Like millions of Europeans, most Jews lived in small villages and had few possessions. But religious discrimination made their lives even more difficult. Jews were not permitted to own land. They could only work in certain professions. They were not allowed to study at the universities or live in most cities unless they were given special permission. And they could not worship as they pleased.

As if all this weren't bad enough, every so often horrible massacres, called "pogroms," took place. "Peasants would . . . fill themselves with vodka, and set out to kill the Jews," remembered the Russian girl from Polotzk, Maryashe, who emigrated to Boston and eventually became Mary Antin, an American writer of the early

Millions of immigrants came to America by ship. The people above are waiting for theirs in the port city of Danzig in 1920.

20th century. "They attacked them with knives and clubs and scythes and axes, killed them or tortured them, and burned their houses."

In many countries, hatred flared among different peoples. Wars broke out; diseases spread and killed millions. For the poor in Europe and Asia, life was not just hard—it was cruel and brutal. To these millions, the lure of a new life in a new country was very tempting.

Why they left: Family stories

Nearly every immigrant came to America for one of three big reasons: economic opportunity, religious freedom, or political liberty. But every immigrant also had his or her own private reasons to leave home, and these reasons are frequently the beginning of a family story.

As you study your family's history, you may bring to light the very personal reasons for your ancestors' departure from their homeland. Here are some examples:

• "Our great-grandfather wanted to live a 'modern' life, and his parents were very traditional. He felt the only way he could fulfill his desire was to move far, far away—to America."

• "I knew that if that no-good brother of mine could succeed in America, so could I."

• "Great-grandma read letters from a relative who had emigrated. They made America sound like a wonderful place."

• "I knew my children would have much more opportunity here than they would ever have in Korea."

• "Great-grandfather heard gold had been discovered in California, and he wanted to strike it rich."

• "I didn't want to go into the Russian army."

• "Great-great-grandpa always wanted a farm of his own. When he heard that in America they were giving land away—free!—to people who agreed to work it, he decided that was for him. He packed his bag that night and left Norway the next morning."

• "My grandmother's best friend was going, and she didn't want to be left behind."

• "My father died during the great influenza epidemic of 1917–18, and my mother decided to take all of us children to live with her brother in America."

• "Great-aunt Tessie heard there was a good job for her in Boston."

• "One of my children was killed in a pogrom. I had three others, and I could not stand the idea of losing them. I wanted to live in a country where pogroms did not exist."

There was also one type of person with a very simple reason:

• "I had no choice in the matter. I was four years old."

The First Wave

The dream of coming to America is not new. Since 1492, when the European Christopher Columbus arrived in North America, people had known about the new land across the sea. Explorers returned to Europe with stories about a place filled with great forests, sparkling rivers, open land, and natives they called "Indians."

This 1609 booklet urged Englishmen to emigrate to America.

By 1600, the first wave of settlers had arrived. Many came temporarily. They trapped beaver and other animals for their fur, and established trade between the "Old World" and America. But these pioneers planned to make their fortunes, then return to Europe to live in comfort. Most were from Spain, France, Holland, and Belgium. Only a few ended up staying for good.

Other groups came to settle permanently in this "New World." Attracted by reports of good, fertile soil, they established their own farms. The great majority of these immigrants were from the British Isles—Scotland and Wales and England. Some sought religious freedom. Others were looking for economic opportunity. Still others came because they wanted political freedom—the right to speak out against the government without fear.

From the 1600s until the late 1700s, America was a colony of the British Empire. Then, in 1776, the American Revolution broke out between colonists and their British rulers. Seven years later, the colonists won and proclaimed a new and free nation. In the Declaration of Independence, the Founding Fathers had said they believed that "all men are created equal." It wasn't clear exactly whom they

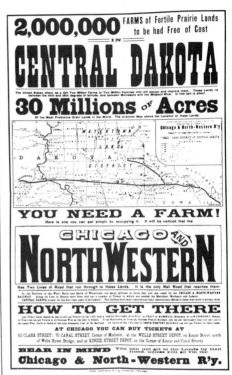

Go West! A railroad company ad tells settlers to move to Dakota.

were talking about—after all, they didn't include women, Native Americans, or African slaves. But they did say their nation was based on freedom and democracy. These principles made America stand out as an inspiration in a world where most nations were ruled by kings and queens.

Word spread throughout the countries of Europe that there were opportunities across the sea. America needed people to build its cities, settle in its wilderness, and work in its factories.

The new nation began to develop over the next few decades. There were no rules restricting who could come, so thousands of immigrants started pouring into the United States. In the years between 1820 and 1880, a second wave of immigrants came. Hundreds of thousands arrived, most of them from Norway, Sweden, Germany, and Ireland. They traveled by

The first Americans

About 30,000 years before an Italian sailor named Cristoforo Colombo "discovered" North America, hundreds of thousands of people were already living on the continent. Today, we call them Native Americans, or Indians.

Scientists believe the first Americans came from Siberia, the part of today's Soviet Union closest to Alaska. We think (no one knows, since there are no written records) that they were Asian peoples searching for new lands.

These wanderers crossed a land bridge that existed at that time between Siberia and Alaska, and moved slowly southward. Over thousands of years, they put down homes all across North America.

By the 1400s, there were probably millions of people living in America. (Some historians believe that when Columbus arrived, 500,000 lived in the eastern part of North America alone.)

They hunted and grew food—maize, pumpkins, and beans—on their own farms. They built shelters, weaved, made pots, and turned animal skins into clothing.

When Europeans began arriving in large ships with white sails, the native peoples were curious. Sometimes there were conflicts, but in many cases the Indians helped the settlers, teaching these "white people" how to catch wild animals and grow plants.

But many settlers saw the natives as obstacles. The Europeans had come a long way for new land, and they didn't want to share it with others. Some purchased land from the natives, but many just took the land and killed any natives who stood in their way. European diseases, which the Indians had no resistance to, killed many more.

Over the next few hundred years, Native American Indians were pushed out of their homelands. Hundreds of thousands were killed in battles with American soldiers and settlers, or forced to move by the new government. Many government promises were made to Indians, and almost all of them have been broken.

Today, some Native Americans live on special reservations that the government set aside. A few million live in cities or towns. And millions of other Americans are descended from marriages between these natives and European settlers.

ship—crowded, unsanitary ships that took weeks to get to America.

These immigrants learned that life in their new country was also difficult, but that it held much more opportunity. Life *felt* freer, too. The settlers wrote to their friends and families to tell them so.

"I am living in God's noble and free soil," a Swedish immigrant who settled in Iowa in 1850 wrote to his family in the Old Country. "I have now been on American soil two and a half years, and I have not been compelled to pay a penny for the privilege of living. Neither is my cap worn out from lifting it in the presence of gentlemen."

Letters like this had a powerful effect on people all over Europe. A family would receive mail from a relative in America. Villagers might gather to hear the letter read, or perhaps a local newspaper would publish it. Soon, everyone was talking about their countryman's great success across the sea.

As interest grew, more information about the New World started appearing. Shipping companies sent representatives to villages across Europe, telling people about the waiting opportunities. Some states in need of a labor force began recruiting through brochures and posters, inviting workers

If it's not home anymore, what is it? The Old Country

The Old Country wasn't just a place; it was people and a way of life.

Three older men are sitting on a porch, reminiscing.

"Ah, things were so tough in the Old Country," says one.

"*Tough?*" says another. "You don't know what the word means. In the Old Country, my father brought up 15 children by working around the clock."

"Listen," says the third. "What kind of nonsense are you talking? Things *weren't* tough in the Old Country." He stops for a minute, then smiles. "Things were *terrible*."

Where are they talking about? No one has even mentioned the name of the country involved. But all of them know exactly what they mean. They're using a famous piece of immigrant shorthand: the expression "the Old Country."

The Old Country was the place an immigrant came from. It wasn't "home" anymore, because most immigrants considered America their home, but it wasn't foreign, either. It was where they had been born, and in many cases where their ancestors had been born, too. Often the immigrants still had family in the Old Country, and they still used the language and the customs they had learned there.

The Old Country didn't necessarily mean a nation. For many people, it brought to mind the little town they lived in, or the farm they remembered fondly—not Italy, or Russia, or Poland, or Austria, but the people, the customs, the good and bad times they had left behind.

Famous early immigrants: The Pilgrims

For hundreds of years, people have been coming to America to escape prejudice and oppression. That was the case with one of the earliest, and most famous, groups of immigrants: the Pilgrims.

The Pilgrims were English men and women who did not agree with the way the Church of England was run. They secretly set up their own separate church, but that was illegal in England, and several of their leaders were jailed.

The "separatists," as they were called, decided that the only way they could pray as they wished was to leave England. In 1608, a group of them sailed over to Holland. They could pray freely in Holland, but they felt like outsiders there.

After hearing about discoveries in the New World, the separatists decided that was the place for them. They secured permission from the King of England to establish a colony in Virginia and arranged to take two sailing ships from Plymouth, England, to North America. One ship, the *Speedwell*, broke down shortly after leaving, so 102 people—68 adults and 34 children—and a crew of 30 ended up jammed onto the second ship, the *Mayflower*.

These travelers spent 66 days at sea before they spotted what is now known as Cape Cod on November 9, 1620. A month later, after exploring the coastline, they established a colony and named it Plymouth, in honor of their town of departure.

When genealogy first became popular in late 19th-century America, many people claimed that they were descended from *Mayflower* passengers. "An Allerton was on the ship," someone might say. "That was my great-great grandfather Allerton."

It was possible, of course. But just having the same last name is *never* proof that anyone is related to you. To clarify exactly who was who, the Society of Mayflower Descendants was founded in the 1880s.

The title of this 1867 painting by Henry Broughton is Pilgrims Going to Church.

Listed below are the names of the original *Mayflower* passengers. If you would like more information about any of these families, you can contact the General Society of Mayflower Descendants, P.O. Box 3297, Plymouth Center, MA 02361; or the New England Historic Genealogical Society, 101 Newbury Street, Boston, MA 02116.

Mayflower Passengers

Alden, John

Allerton, Isaac, his wife Mary, and their three children Bartholomew, Remember, and Mary

Allerton, John, a seaman

Billington, John, his wife Eleanor, and two sons John and Francis

Bradford, William, and his wife Dorothy May

Brewster, William and Mary, and their two sons Love and Wrestling

Britteridge, Richard

Brown, Peter

Butten, William,** servant to Samuel Fuller

Cartier, Robert, a servant to the Mullins family

Carver, John, and his wife Katherine

Chilton, James, his wife, and their daughter Mary

Clarke, Richard

Cooke, Francis, and his son John

Crakston, John, and his son John

Doty, Edward, a servant of the Hopkins family

Eaton, Francis, his wife Sarah, and their son Samuel

English, Thomas, a seaman

Fletcher, Moses

Fuller, Edward, his wife Ann, and their son Samuel

Fuller, Samuel

Gardiner, Richard

Goodman, John

Holbeck, William, a servant to the White family

Hooke, John, boy servant to Isaac Allerton

Hopkins, Steven and Elizabeth, and Steven's two children from a previous marriage, Giles and Constance, and two children with Elizabeth, Damaris and Oceanus*

Howland, John, a servant

Langemore, John, a servant to the Martin family

Latham, William, a boy servant

Leitster, Edward, a servant of the Hopkins family

Margeson, Edmond

Martin, Christopher, and his wife

Minter, Desire, a maid

More, Ellen, a little girl

More, Jasper, a boy

More, Richard, a boy

More, —, a boy

Mullins, William, his wife Alice, and their two children Joseph and Priscilla

Priest, Degory

Prower, Solomon, a servant to the Martin family

Rigdale, John, and his wife Alice

Rogers, Thomas, and his son Joseph

Soule, George, a servant of the Winslow family

Standish, Myles, and his wife Rose

Story, Elias, a servant of the Winslow family

Thompson, Edward, a servant of the White family

Tilly, Edward, his wife Ann, and two children who were their cousins, Henry Sampson and Humility Cooper

Tilly, John, his wife, and their daughter Elizabeth

Tinker, Thomas, his wife, and a son

Turner, John, and two sons

Unidentified maid servant

Warren, Richard

White, William and Susana, and their sons, Resolved and Peregrine

Wilder, Roger, a servant

Williams, Thomas

Winslow, Edward, and his wife Elizabeth

Winslow, Gilbert

---

*born at sea   **died at sea

to come over. Local newspapers gave immigrants advice about the easiest way to leave for America. Tickets were mailed by relatives to other members of a family so that they could follow as quickly as possible.

Before long, millions of Europeans were on their way to America.

The Young Nation Expands

The country these immigrants arrived in had changed a great deal since the first settlers reached its untamed shores in the 1600s. Now there were busy, bustling cities like New York, Boston, New Orleans, and Philadelphia. By 1850, steamboats were whistling up and down American rivers. The northern states had factories and mills. The southern states also had vast, rich farms where much of the work was done by slaves who had been kidnapped in Africa and brought here.

America was expanding. At first, newcomers settled along the eastern coast of the new nation. Practically the only people living in the lands to the west were Native Americans, the "Indians." But settlers began exploring the land, and by the 1840s, thousands of pioneers were moving west to

The American West looked like a giant, open wonderland. This lithograph was made in 1870; millions of settlers would come over the next few decades.

homestead and start a new life.

Then in 1848, a discovery was made near Sacramento, California. Word spread that gold had been found near John Sutter's sawmill, and by 1849 people from all over the world were flooding into the area. So many prospectors came with dreams of striking it rich that this period is known as "The Gold Rush."

Among the people who came were large numbers of Chinese workers, many from Canton province in the south of China. They stayed to work in the San Francisco area or on the building of the transcontinental railroad.

Beginning in the 1840s, many families headed north and west following a path called "The Oregon Trail." They weren't looking for instant riches—they just wanted to settle their families in the fertile Oregon valleys. It's a good thing they were patient. The trek by covered wagon took anywhere from four to six months.

While the population began to move westward, the nation grew richer. Scientific advances like the cotton gin and the steam engine were turning the United States into an industrial power. American ships were sailing the seas and transporting goods everywhere.

Then, from 1861 to 1865, the bloody American Civil War was fought. Few immigrants entered the United States during these years. After the war ended, however, immigration once again picked up.

Before the 1860s, most people came to the United States on sailing boats. A ship leaving Hamburg, Germany, might take eight weeks to arrive. But by the 1880s, steamships were traveling across the ocean in half the time, or less, than it had taken sailing ships. The trip was easier and healthier; and because ships could travel more quickly, more trips could be made per ship.

By the 1890s, the arrival of a few thousand immigrants each year had turned into a mighty wave of millions. Some came from Mexico, Canada, and the Caribbean, and a good number came from northern Europe. But most

A sod house on the old prairie in 1885. This immigrant family built their house out of packed mud near Miller, South Dakota.

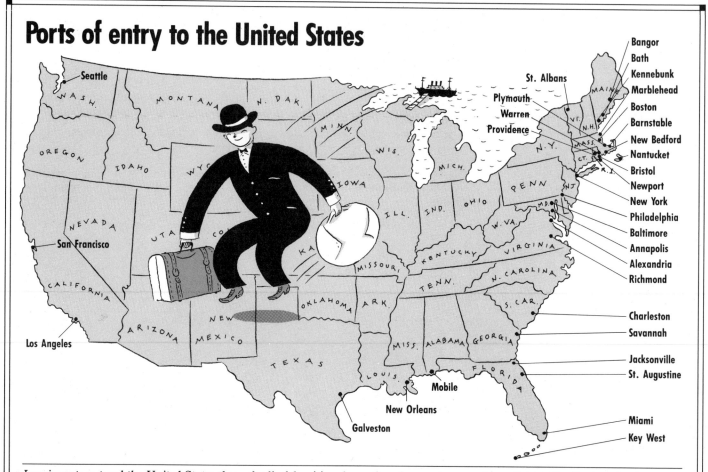

Ports of entry to the United States

Seattle

WASH.

OREGON

MONTANA

IDAHO

N. DAK.

MINN.

WIS.

MICH.

IOWA

WYO.

NEVADA

UTAH

COL.

KAN.

MISSOURI

San Francisco

CALIFORNIA

ARIZONA

NEW MEXICO

Los Angeles

TEXAS

OKLAHOMA

ARK.

LOUIS.

ILL.

IND.

OHIO

KENTUCKY

TENN.

MISS.

ALABAMA

GEORGIA

N. CAROLINA

S. CAR.

PENN.

N.J.

MD.

W. VA.

VIRGINIA

FLORIDA

N.Y.

VT.

N.H.

MASS.

CT.

R.I.

MAINE

Galveston

New Orleans

Mobile

St. Albans

Plymouth

Warren

Providence

Bangor

Bath

Kennebunk

Marblehead

Boston

Barnstable

New Bedford

Nantucket

Bristol

Newport

New York

Philadelphia

Baltimore

Annapolis

Alexandria

Richmond

Charleston

Savannah

Jacksonville

St. Augustine

Miami

Key West

Immigrants entered the United States through all of the cities above, though some processed very few people. Copies of passenger lists for these places are in the National Archives in Washington, D.C., or its regional offices (see Appendix).

immigrants came from the poorer lands of southern and eastern Europe.

The year 1907 marked the peak of immigration. An average of 3,000 people entered the United States every day of that year. By December 31, over 1,285,000 people had immigrated—a record that stands to this day.

Not everyone was happy about this latest wave of immigration. Before the 1880s, most immigrants had come from countries in northern and western Europe, and they didn't like the "new" immigrants from southern and eastern Europe because their customs and languages were so different.

American workers were also concerned. Would these newcomers work for less money, and take jobs away from them? A debate about who should be admitted began in the 1880s and went on until the 1920s. In 1914, however, these arguments were put aside when war exploded in Europe. It was called "The Great War" because so many countries took part—including the United States, which entered in 1917. For four years, very few people sailed the seas or came to America.

But while the rest of the world stayed put, there was a giant movement inside America. Black Americans began leaving their homes in the rural South for the big cities in the North. This movement was known as "The Great Migration." From 1916 through 1919, as many as 500,000 blacks moved to northern industrial cities such as Pittsburgh, Detroit, Philadelphia, Cleveland, and New York City. Like so many immigrants before and after them, they were looking for work, opportunity, and an escape from prejudice.

In 1918, World War I ended. The wave of immigration began to rise again in mighty numbers. In 1921,

Working your way over: The story of indentured servants

To a poor boy or girl growing up in England or Scotland or Wales in the 1700s, America sounded like an exciting place. But the cost of a trip on a clipper ship was very expensive, and few could afford to pay their way.

In America at the same time, there were well-off English families who needed servants. They couldn't find anyone to work for them, however, because there were so few English men and women in the colonies.

A new kind of immigration, "indentured servitude," was born from these two situations. An "indenture" was a contract obliging an immigrant to work for a family—without a salary—for a specified number of years in exchange for the cost of the immigrant's passage. Most of these contracts bound an adult indentured servant to four years of service; teenagers were expected to work without salary until they turned 21. Maybe as many as 50 percent of the English men and women who came to America in its early days were under this type of labor contract.

Some indentured servants had arrangements with families before they left. Others met their families when they arrived. In those cases, the ship's captain would hold an auction at the port where they landed. Each servant would be offered ("Margaret, 19 years old, kitchen maid") to the highest bidder.

John, a 20-year-old Englishman, made an agreement with the Jones family of Virginia before he left England. He would work for them for four years in exchange for the price of his ticket over. In 1754, after a four-week trip, John's ship sailed into Roanoke, Virginia. He was met there by Mr. Jones, who took the servant to the Jones's home in Williamsburg. For the next four years, John worked as a coach driver and butler. His only pay was a place to sleep, clothing, and food.

When John's term was up, the Jones family gave him a small sum of money and a new suit of clothes (some families also gave a small piece of land). John could now live and work anywhere he wanted.

Indentured servitude continued in the United States until the 1820s.

The debate over closing the door to America

Most Americans are proud of our reputation as the greatest immigrant nation in the world. But throughout U.S. history, heated debates have raged about immigration. Time and again, groups have mounted campaigns to have the doors to this country closed, if not to all immigrants, then at least to all of a certain group.

These cries for exclusion came mainly from two groups. American laborers were afraid of losing their jobs. They feared that bosses would fire Americans and hire new immigrants, who would work for lower wages. This was the main reason that a law was passed in 1885 prohibiting immigrants from coming to America with a job already in hand.

The second anti-immigration group believed that newcomers were "inferior." They wanted to have these immigrants excluded to "protect" American civilization.

Until the 1870s, there were no restrictions on immigration to this country. Over the next decade, barriers went up to exclude certain types of people, like convicts and people "likely to become a public charge" (those who looked like they would not be able to support themselves financially).

In 1882, the first law was passed banning people from a specific country. The Chinese Exclusion Act suspended the right of workers from China to come to the United States. This ugly law was passed to satisfy angry white settlers who worried that the Chinese would take away their jobs by working for lower pay. The only Chinese still eligible to enter were students, tourists, and businessmen—a class that included very few.

The Chinese Exclusion Act marked the beginning of a new era in American history. Over the next 40 years, bill after bill was introduced in Congress to stop the flow of immigrants.

These bills made their way into law slowly, almost piece by piece. In 1903, political radicals were excluded. In 1907, a "gentleman's agreement" between the United States and Japan barred Japanese immigration. In 1917, a bill that had been introduced many times over the previous 20 years— banning people who could not read or write—was finally passed over the veto of President Woodrow Wilson. By 1917, there were 33 categories of people who could not enter the United States.

The next step was to exclude poor immigrants from southern and eastern Europe. The anti-immigration forces suggested laws creating quotas, which would limit the number of people who could come to the United States from each country. In 1921, a law was passed that allowed more immigration from western Europe—which was no longer sending many people to America—and severely limited immigration from southern and eastern Europe. Under the National Origins Act of 1924, even more severe quotas were established for those countries.

As many as 100,000 Italians had come in one year during the early 1900s. Now the quota was 5,802 a year. Millions had come from Russia, but the United States would now accept only 2,784 a year. Greeks had immigrated by the thousands. Under the new quota, only 307 could come yearly.

For the next 40 years, those quotas were in effect. Few western European countries ever met their quota; every eastern and southern European country exceeded it in normal years.

Finally, in 1965, that quota law was repealed and a new system was put into effect. It established more even-handed numbers for countries from all over the world and made exceptions for political refugees and people who had relatives already in the United States.

Today, immigration is once again flourishing. The number of immigrants admitted to the United States in 1991 is comparable to the numbers that arrived during the high-tide years of the early 1900s. There are still restrictions —and still debates over who should be admitted—but today the United States is once again a nation with an open door.

more than 600,000 arrived.

And then, the wave was stopped. Laws were passed by Congress to severely restrict entry into the United States and to fix quotas for each country. For the next 40 years, few immigrants were admitted. The terrible economic upheaval of the 1930s, which was called "The Great Depression," played a role in that. So did the horribly destructive Second World War (1939 to 1945), in which millions of young people from nearly every nation on earth fought and died. But even after World War II was over, American immigration laws kept out many who wanted to enter.

The Newest Immigrants

It wasn't until 1965 that things changed. In that year, President Lyndon Johnson signed a new immigration law, changing the quota system to a more evenly distributed one for all nations. Emphasis was also placed on uniting Americans with family members from overseas.

People still journeyed from countries that had been part of the great tide of immigration of the early 1900s. But now thousands were also coming from new lands. The greatest number left South America and the Caribbean.

Their reasons were similar to those of earlier settlers: Some came fleeing harsh governments, hoping to find freedom; others came for economic opportunity; and many came for a combination of these reasons.

Thousands more arrived from Asia—from India, Pakistan, Taiwan, Korea, Cambodia, Laos, and Vietnam. They came because quotas no longer kept them out, and because jet travel had cut dramatically the time it took to get here. But most of all, they came because their countries were poor and they wanted to reach for the same economic opportunity that had attracted millions of immigrants before them.

The United States is once more a country willing to embrace people from all over the world. There are still long waiting lists, and not everyone who wishes to enter will be able to. But the dream and promise of America is once again offered to people from many different lands.

For hundreds of years, families have made history by coming to these shores, bringing with them their own special customs, skills, hopes, dreams, and history.

And over the course of those two centuries, millions of immigrants, most of them poor, changed the United States from a small, underpopulated little country into a huge nation made up of people from every corner of the earth.

A Cuban refugee arriving in Miami shows his joy by kissing the ground, 1960.

Involuntary Americans: The Africans

African people arrived in America before the *Mayflower* did. But unlike the *Mayflower* passengers—and nearly all other immigrants to America—they did not choose to come here. They were kidnapped.

In 1619, a ship arrived in Jamestown, Virginia, with 20 Africans in its hold. These first Africans to set foot in North America were slaves sold at auction to early settlers.

Over the next 200 years, British, Portuguese, Spanish, and other ships wandered up and down the coast of West Africa, capturing Africans who lived in what today are the nations of Senegal, Ghana, Gambia, Liberia, Benin (Dahomey), Togo, Nigeria, and the Ivory Coast. The tribes they came from included the Ashanti, Bantu, Ibo, Mandingo, Efik, Kru, Dahomean, Hausa, and Fanti.

The youngest and strongest of these captives were stuffed into the slave ships' dark, hot cargo holds. Although many immigrant groups traveled to America under terrible conditions, no other group faced the horrors that were routine for Africans. Some say as many

as 40 million were brought to the Western Hemisphere in this fashion—and some say 20 million died on the trip over.

Africans were brought here primarily to work in the fields and great houses of the southeastern United States. They lived in small shacks on the grounds of the plantations.

African men and women were treated as property; they could be bought and sold by their owners, who forced them to give up their names and identities. Families were broken up when the owner wished to sell a child or a parent to another owner.

When slavery was finally outlawed throughout the United States after the Civil War, African-Americans, though liberated, had few possessions or skills. Many stayed in the South. When millions moved to the cities of the North in the early years of the 20th century, they again encountered prejudice and discrimination. Years of struggle—including the famous civil rights movement of the 1950s and '60s—slowly eliminated laws that made prejudice legal. Attitudes, however, have changed far more slowly.

Slaves were *not* immigrants, and the way in which they were brought to America still echoes powerfully in the lives of their descendants. But like the groups that came to this land after them, African-Americans have struggled to make it in America, and they boast millions of success stories.

CHAPTER THREE

Finding Your Families

BEGINNING YOUR GENEALOGICAL SEARCH

Sometime in that great parade of American immigration, *your* family arrived. Your ancestors made a long and difficult journey through space to get to this country. Now you are about to make a journey through time to find them. Your trip will be easier, less expensive—and a lot more fun.

You are going to become an Ancestor Detector. You will work backward into the past from what you already know to what you want to know—just like a detective. You will be collecting data, looking for clues, following up tips and snips of information. Eventually, the clues will lead you to exciting discoveries.

"You won't be able to find much," someone in your family may say. "Our ancestors came from a country where very few records were kept."

"I doubt you'll get far," someone else might warn. "No one really remembers very much about where our family came from."

Another family member may tell you, "The records that did exist are gone; they were destroyed during World War II."

Those are all reasonable points. Happily, however, they are not always true. One of the great joys of genealogy is showing family members that what they think is impossible—finding pieces of your past—really *is* possible. Someone in your family may remember more than anyone knows. And a surprising number of old records do exist—in the United States and in other countries, too.

You've started on a jigsaw puzzle for a lifetime, because genealogy is a hobby that never ends. You can work on it for a while, then leave it for weeks or even months. But looking into your family's past is thrilling, and there's always more to learn. You'll come back to it time and again.

It won't always be easy, however. You might pursue a certain piece of

A government inspector at work. This immigrant family has just landed at Kennedy Airport in New York City and is having its entry papers checked. When and where did your family arrive in the United States?

your puzzle for a very long time, following all the leads, doing everything exactly right—and come up with nothing. There will be times when you won't have a clue as to what to do next.

But there will also be rewarding times. One day you might uncover a piece of information—something you've been trying to verify over months or even years—and suddenly a whole section of the puzzle will fall into place.

Most importantly, there will be unforgettable moments. Imagine digging up a wonderful story about your grandfather's childhood, or learning about how your family played a part in a famous event. Just think of what it would be like to read a note one of your ancestors actually wrote a hundred years ago.

Start at the Very Beginning

Your own long and fascinating history is waiting to be discovered. But exactly how do you begin to unearth your family's secrets? Genealogy is as easy as 1-2-3:

1. Gather all the facts you know or can easily find out about your family. By talking to relatives, you will locate lots of information about your past. You might also discover that they have documents that will lead you to more information.

2. Organize what you discover. Put all your information in one place, arranged so that you can find it easily and refer to it. Make sure everything is accurate.

3. Find new information. Look for new sources of information. Make sure any new information is accurate, also. Then write it down in your own record books.

The idea is to get the information people already know, organize it, make sure it's true, and then add to it.

You don't need any fancy equipment. A loose-leaf notebook, copies of the charts in the Appendix, and a pencil will get you off to a fine start.

Now, for the very first step. An

important rule in genealogy is this: Go from the known to the unknown. Let what you know lead you to what you don't know. What you know about your own life will lead you to information about your parents' lives. Facts about your parents' lives will give you clues to your grandparents' lives. In this way, you will delve deeper and deeper into the past.

You won't begin your search for the past in a library, in a government records center, or in interviews with family members. You'll start gathering the facts from the person you know best: yourself.

At the top of a piece of loose-leaf paper, write HISTORY OF (your name). Then write the facts of your life. Answer these questions—or at least, answer as many of them as you can:

● What is your full name? Whom were you named after?

● When were you born? Where?

● What are your parents' full names? When were they born, and where? When and where were they married? What kind of work does your father do? Your mother?

● Where do you live now? Where else have you lived?

● Do you have any brothers or sisters? Name them. When and where were they born? After whom were they named?

● Who are your grandparents? Where do they live? When and where were they born? After whom were they named? When and where did they get married? What kind of work do (or did) they do?

● Do you know the names of any of your great-grandparents? If so, note them—and leave room for the dates and places of their birth, marriage, and death.

When you finish, examine your first genealogical record—carefully. What information are you not 100 percent sure about? (Make a note by putting a question mark next to these answers.) What information is missing?

Have your mother or father check your answers to be sure that there are no mistakes, and ask them to help you fill in any missing information.

Now you're ready to transfer all the

information onto your first genealogical chart. This is the most convenient way to keep track of your ancestors.

Genealogists have designed special charts that help you see at a glance what you know and don't know about your family's history. They are given many names—pedigrees, lineage charts, family diagrams, and family trees.

Some charts are drawn in complex designs, like ornate pictures of real trees with hundreds of branches. Other charts may be simple but enormous, with nothing more than lots of lines and words connecting across a sheet of paper.

Pedigree charts are not exactly the same as family trees. Pedigrees trace an individual's *direct* ancestors. That means only parents and children—no uncles and aunts, cousins, and so on. Family trees may include the *extended family* (all of those uncles, aunts, cousins, etc.) and can be quite huge. Today, with the help of computers, people can draw and redraw trees that include thousands of names.

Even in their simplest form, it's easy to see how these charts got the name of "tree." After all, they do have branches, they display family roots, and they grow for hundreds of years.

This 1817 family tree shows the seven children of Job Dennen and Lucy Gott.

Pedigree Chart

16 AARON WOLFMAN
8 Born: 1850(?)
Place: LAPIZ, RUSSIA
Married:
Place:
Died: c. 1921
Place: LAPIZ, RUSSIA
17
18 SLAVA SHAPIRO
9 Born:
Place:
Died:
Place:
19

4 MORRIS WOLFMAN
Born: 25 NOV 1881
Place: LAPIZ, RUSSIA
Married: 26 MAR 1909
Place: BROOKLYN, NY
Died: 22 JAN 1964
Place: BROOKLYN, NY

2 AARON WOLFMAN
Born: 7 FEB 1922
Place: BROOKLYN, NY
Married: 4 APR 1948
Place: BROOKLYN, NY
Died:
Place:

5 IDA FUDELOWICZ
Born: 1885 (?)
Place: SZRENSK, MLAWA, Rus Pland
Died: 23 FEB 1972
Place: QUEENS, NEW YORK

10 MENDEL FUDELOWICZ
Born: 10 JAN 1860
Place: SZRENSK, MLAWA Rus PL
Married: 1884?
Place: SZRENSK, MLAWA, Rus PL
Died: 17 JAN 1947
Place: BROOKLYN, NY

20 BEREK FUDELOWICZ
21 BLIMA NORDENBERG

11 SHEINA MIESIAC
Born: 15 APR 1857
Place: RAZANOW, Rus PL
Died: 9 MAR 1948
Place: BROOKLYN, NY

22 A MIESIAC
23 SURA RADZANOWICZ

1 IRA WOLFMAN
Born: 7 OCT 1950
Place: BROOKLYN, NY
Married: 24 JUNE 1979
Place: WESTCHESTER, NY
Died:
Place:
Spouse: JULIA DIAMANT

12 ISRAEL PERLO
Born:
Place:
Married:
Place:
Died:
Place: LOMZA, RUS PL

24
25
26 BEYLA SHILEPSKI
13 Born:
Place:
Died: c. 1924
Place:
27

6 HYMEN PERLO
Born: 22 JAN 1894
Place: LOMZA RUSSIAN POLAND
Married: 31 JULY 1920
Place: BROOKLYN, NY
Died: 4 JAN 1955
Place: BROOKLYN, NY

3 BEATRICE PERLO
Born: 2 MAY 1925
Place: BROOKLYN, NY
Died:
Place:

14 CHAIM BURSTEIN
Born:
Place:
Married:
Place: LOMZA, Rus PLAND
Died: c 1922
Place: ZAMBROW, Rus PL

28
29

7 EDNA BURSTEIN
Born: 1896?
Place: ZAMBROW RUSSIA-POLAND
Died: 7 AUG 1963
Place: QUEENS, NY

15 TSIVYA APPEL
Born:
Place:
Died: 1898(?)
Place: ZAMBROW RUS-POLAND

30
31

PERSON SUBMITTING PEDIGREE CHART: IRA WOLFMAN

Person Number 1 on this chart is the same as Person Number _____ on Chart Number _____.

A Pedigree Chart

Start with a Pedigree Chart of your direct ancestors: your parents, your parents' parents, your grandparents' parents, and so on. With this chart, you will be able to see at a glance the men and women you are descended from. Remember that if *any* of your direct ancestors had not existed, *you* would never have been born.

Make several copies of the blank Pedigree Chart in the Appendix. Enter all information carefully, legibly, and in pencil. As you continue your research and information gathering, you'll discover new facts that will make it necessary to revise your charts. You don't want to have to rewrite an entire page because a few facts have changed.

Before you start filling in the chart, mind this simple genealogical rule when writing down dates: Always put the day first, write out the month second, and the full year third. For example, 25 June 1847 and 30 January 1978.

This rule avoids confusion. The shorter method can lead to mistakes: Does 6/11/86 mean June 11, 1986, or November 6, 1886?

Begin filling in your chart. At the far left-hand corner, write your name next to Number 1. At "Born," write your date of birth. Next to "Place," write where you were born, including the town and state or country: Albany, New York; London, England; Helena, Montana; or Lomza, Poland, for instance.

If you know the county or province of a birthplace, write that down, too. This will make it easier to locate a small town. For example, Bedford, Taylor County, Iowa, is easier to find than simply Bedford, Iowa, would be. This is especially true with common names—there are *three* villages in Ohio called Oakwood. So whenever you can, indicate the county.

After you've filled in your personal information, do the same for your parents. Write your father's name next to Number 2, and next to Number 3 write your mother's first and maiden name (her last name *before* she was married). This numbering pattern—even numbers (2,4,6,8) for men and odd numbers (3,5,7,9) for women—is the way to keep all your genealogical records. (The only exception to the odd/even rule is for Number 1. Put yourself there whether you're male or

---

Where do you put extra ancestors?

If you manage to trace your family very far back, you won't be able to fit all the generations on one chart.

But on any Pedigree Chart, you can add a note that says, "Number 1 on this chart is Number _____ on Chart # _____." This is called a "cross-reference," and it's the key to keeping your records in order.

So if you find an ancestor who goes back further than the spaces in your chart, just expand to another page.

Say you discover information about Number 16 (your great-great-grandfather) that leads you to *his* father. You could then put great-great-grandpa at spot Number 1 on another chart, which you'd label Chart Number 2. Your new discovery (great-great-great-grandpa) would be written in at the Number 2 spot.

And at the bottom of the new chart, you'd write, "Number 1 on this chart is Number 16 on Chart Number 1."

Family Group Sheet

FUDALOWICZ FAMILY (handwritten)

HUSBAND MENDEL NASIEK FELD (born FUDALOWICZ)	WIFE Sheina Rudila MIESIAC
Born 10 JAN 1860 Place SZRENSK, RUS-POLAND [1]	Born 15 APR 1857 Place RADZANOW, RUS-POL [2]
Married Place	—
Died 17 JAN 1947 Place BROOKLYN, NY [3]	Died 9 MAR 1948 Place BROOKLYN NY [4]
Buried 17 JAN 1947 Place BARON Hirsch Cemetery, S.I, N.Y. [3]	Buried 10 MAR 1948 Place BARON Hirsch Cemetery, S.I. NY [4]
Husband's Father BEREK FUDALOWICZ [1]	Wife's Father Abram MIESIAC [2]
Husband's Mother BLIMA NORDENBERG [1]	Wife's Mother Sura Dwojra RADZANOWICZ [2]
Husband's Other Wives	Wife's Other Husbands

CHILDREN Last Name, First Name, Middle Name, Nickname or Other	WHEN BORN Day/Month/Year	WHERE BORN Town/County/State	DATE OF FIRST MARRIAGE To Whom	WHEN DIED Day/Month/Year
FUDALOWICZ, IDA "Ajdla"	1885 [2]	SZRENSK, MLAWA, POL	26 MAR 1909 MORRIS WOLFMAN	23 FEB 1972 [3] / 22 JAN 1964 [4]

Sources of Information
1) Birth certificate, Ira Wolfman possession via LDS Library
2) MEL HAMBERG documents
3) and 4) Death certificates, Ira Wolfman possession, NYC Dept of Health

female.) List every woman under her maiden (unmarried) name.

Under your parents' names, write their dates and places of birth. The date and place of your parents' marriage is listed under your father's information.

By the time you come to your grandparents (numbers 4 to 7), even your parents may not have all the answers. And when you reach your great-grandparents (8 to 15), there will almost certainly be gaps of information. You probably won't know some of the names for these slots—especially the maiden names of your great-grandmothers.

In your genealogical hunt, you will be adding to this Pedigree Chart all the time. Make photocopies of the one you've just filled in, and keep them with your loose-leaf notebook.

A Family Group Sheet

Another useful chart for genealogists is the Family Group Sheet, which is used to organize information about all the members of your family, including the many you cannot fit onto your Pedigree Chart. Sisters, brothers, cousins, uncles, aunts, great-uncles and great-aunts are not direct ancestors, so their records should be en-

Branching out: Unusual family trees

Family trees can be displayed in many creative ways. People don't just write them down. They sew them, draw them, paint, crochet, appliqué, embroider, and computerize them.

There are photo family trees, using pictures of each generation. There are calligraphy trees, made out of the names of all the family members.

In a booklet called "The Living Family Tree," Marie Schreiner offers suggestions for unusual family trees. Among her ideas:

• **Artifact tree.** Make a tree using items that relate to each person: a lock of hair, a fingerprint, a baby tooth.

• **Meaningful-shape tree.** A family tree doesn't have to look like a tree. Why not use a shape that reflects your family? The Schreiners used organ pipes to list their names. Marie suggests books on a shelf for a family of avid readers, or an airplane outline for the family of a pilot.

• **"Palm" tree.** Maryloo Stephens created a tree out of 81 handprints. Relatives sent tracings of their hands to her, and Maryloo cut out the shapes, using a different shade of blue fabric for each generation. She embroi-

dered the name of the hand's owner on each print, and added a number indicating the order of birth.

The handprints were then attached to a tree trunk, which Maryloo appliquéd and placed on a quilt. This quilt was presented to Maryloo's mother and father as a gift for their sixtieth wedding anniversary.

Other projects include a popsicle stick tree, a cross-stitch tree, and several family tree quilts. If you'd like a copy of the booklet, write to Marie Schreiner, 2709 Lamplighter Lane, Minneapolis, MN 55422.

tered on these sheets.

Make up one Family Group Sheet for every "nuclear family"—that is, each group of husband, wife, and children. The family name should be written in large letters at the top of the page, followed by the husband's name, with all his information on the lines directly below. Place the wife's name and her information on the designated lines. Below, place the names of each child of that marriage.

Fill in the Family Group Sheet for your father, mother, any brothers or sisters, and yourself. When you come to the "Children" section, start with the firstborn in your family. Then list the other children in order of birth, down to the youngest. Names—including your own—should be written last name, first name, middle name, and then any other given names or nicknames.

Every member of your family should end up on at least one group sheet. Some will be on two—one as a child, then another when they have their own families.

You don't have to use this particular Family Group Sheet. Maybe you want to include baptism, communion, bar mitzvah, or other religious ceremony dates. You might even want to include

Reading a relationship chart

	1	**2**	**3**	**4**	**5**	**6**
COMMON ANCESTOR	CHILD	GRAND-CHILD	GREAT-GRAND-CHILD	G-G-GRAND-CHILD	G-G-G-GRAND-CHILD	4G-GRAND-CHILD
1 CHILD	BROTHER/SISTER	NEPHEW/NIECE	GRAND-NEPHEW/NIECE	GREAT-GRAND-NEPHEW/NIECE	G-G-GRAND-NEPHEW/NIECE	G-G-G-GRAND-NEPHEW/NIECE
2 GRAND-CHILD	NEPHEW/NIECE	1ST COUSIN	1ST COUSIN ONCE REMOVED	1ST COUSIN TWICE REMOVED	1ST COUSIN 3X REMOVED	1ST COUSIN 4X REMOVED
3 GREAT-GRAND-CHILD	GRAND-NEPHEW/NIECE	1ST COUSIN ONCE REMOVED	2ND COUSIN	2ND COUSIN ONCE REMOVED	2ND COUSIN TWICE REMOVED	2ND COUSIN 3X REMOVED
4 G-G-GRAND-CHILD	GREAT-GRAND-NEPHEW/NIECE	1ST COUSIN TWICE REMOVED	2ND COUSIN ONCE REMOVED	3RD COUSIN	3RD COUSIN ONCE REMOVED	3RD COUSIN TWICE REMOVED
5 G-G-G-GRAND-CHILD	G-G-GRAND-NEPHEW/NIECE	1ST COUSIN 3X REMOVED	2ND COUSIN TWICE REMOVED	3RD COUSIN ONCE REMOVED	4TH COUSIN	4TH COUSIN ONCE REMOVED
6 4G-GRAND-CHILD	G-G-G-GRAND-NEPHEW/NIECE	1ST COUSIN 4X REMOVED	2ND COUSIN 3X REMOVED	3RD COUSIN TWICE REMOVED	4TH COUSIN ONCE REMOVED	5TH COUSIN

Did you ever wonder what a second cousin was? Or a first cousin, once removed? How do you get a cousin removed, anyway? And can you get a second cousin, once removed, moved a second time? These terms are a shorthand way of explaining how you are connected to other relatives.

The chart to the right helps you figure out what your relationships would be called if you wanted to be formal. The directions for reading the chart follow below. But first, you have to understand what "second" and "third" and "removed" mean.

Cousin is a term for any relative who is descended from a common ancestor with you but who is not a sister or brother. The children of your parents' brothers and sisters are your cousins. So are the children of your parents' cousins. But one is a first cousin, and one is a second cousin.

A *first cousin* is someone who has two of the same grandparents as you do. A *second cousin* is someone who has the same *great*-grandparents. As you go further back, the relationship becomes more distant. So your *third cousin* is someone whose *great-great*-grandparents are the same as yours. You probably even have eighth and ninth cousins somewhere.

Removed means that you and your relative are from different generations. Someone *once removed* would be a child of your grandparents' siblings. For example: My father's first cousin is my first cousin, once removed. My grandfather's first cousin is my first cousin, twice removed.

Here's how the chart works:

1. Figure out what relative ("X") you have in common with another relative.
2. Find your relationship to "X" in the far left-hand column.
3. Have your relative find his or her relationship to "X" in the very top column.
4. Now figure out where both of your columns meet. That's the formal term for *your* relationship.
Example: Sharon and Evie are both related to Ida. Sharon is Ida's granddaughter (far left column, number 2). Evie is Ida's great-granddaughter (top column, number 3). Sharon and Evie are first cousins, once removed.

Logging it in

You may want to set up an address log. This is a list of every address where a family lived, and the dates they lived there.

Set up the record so that there is plenty of room to write in new addresses for every few years. Addresses that have been forgotten can be found on many documents—birth certificates, marriage licenses, wills, etc. Perhaps you will find letters that your parents or grandparents saved or old phone books and city directories, which many local libraries carry.

Next to the date and the address, write where you got the information. This "Source" column is very important. You must keep track of where every bit of information comes from because you may get conflicting information later. Knowing where you got

the data will help you decide which is more trustworthy. A good place to keep this log is on the back of the Family Group Sheet.

In the case below, I had a number of different addresses for my mother's parents between 1915 and 1955.

Hymen Perlo Family Address Log

DATE	ADDRESS	SOURCE
Jan. 1915	256 Dumont Ave, Brooklyn, NY	Hymen Perlo's declaration (above)
Dec. 1919	250 Amboy St., Bklyn	H. Perlo's petition (above)
May 1925	212 Sutter Ave., Bklyn	Beatrice Perlo's birth certificate
1926-27	88 Newport St, Bklyn	Recollection, Sylvia Perlo Elliott
1933	2202 Douglas St., Bklyn	Polk Bklyn. Directory, Vol. 90
1948	90 Blake Ave., Bklyn	Marriage certificate Bea Perlo Wolfman
1955	90 Blake Ave., Bklyn.	Death certificate, Hymen Perlo

a physical description or a photograph. Use the back of the sample sheet for those kinds of things—or design your own Family Group Sheet. Just be sure to use the same style throughout.

Keep all your Family Group Sheets together in your loose-leaf book. Group them according to last name, and keep them in chronological order—either oldest or youngest family on top, followed by the rest in order. That will make it easier to find them.

And you *will* need them. These sheets are where you are going to keep much of the information you find. Later, you can use the information on them to make other Pedigree Charts and family trees.

CHAPTER FOUR

Coming to America

THE IMMIGRANT ADVENTURE BEGINS

L ife in the Old Country may have been terrible. And life in America may have sounded wonderful. But in spite of all that, leaving home was *never* easy.

Imagine what it would have been like to leave your homeland forever, and what it would have felt like if *you* had to make the decision.

You wake up one morning and say goodbye to everything you've known. Goodbye to your parents. Your friends. Goodbye to the familiar streets you have come to know so well. Goodbye to the music and food you have grown up with, and to the language you speak.

You travel a long distance—on foot,

The Border at Brody, Austria. In the early 1900s, Russian emigrants sneaked across here on their way to America.

perhaps, or by horse-drawn buggy, bus, or railroad. After a long while, you arrive in a very busy city, a place you have never seen before. You make your way to the harbor. You stand on endless lines with thousands of other people. You already feel exhausted. All around, you hear sounds of confusion, excitement, and fear.

You have bought a ticket, paying what to you is an enormous sum of money. "For that much money, our family could have eaten well for a month," you think. In fact, your entire family scrimped and saved for many months so that you could afford to leave your homeland.

You already had to wait for weeks, maybe even months, to get the permits to leave your village. Now you have to wait even longer. You sit in the harbor town, impatient. A day passes, maybe two or three.

Finally, you are permitted to board a ship. Nearly 2,000 passengers come with you. A few, well-off passengers have private cabins on the highest decks, but most people—including you—must head down to the lowest deck. It is called "steerage" because this is where the ship's steering machinery is kept.

As you descend, you hear people's voices everywhere; your head throbs with the different languages and sounds. You finally reach the room you will sleep in, and you notice it is dark and huge and windowless—with nearly 200 beds. You claim the top of a double bunk and place your heavy suitcase on the bed, knowing you will probably end up sleeping with it—there is no place for storage.

You head back to the top deck for

Not everyone came to the U.S.A.

During the 19th and early 20th centuries, more than 60 million people left their homelands for other countries. One out of every four did *not* come to the United States. They went instead to other countries with large immigrant populations. Argentina, Australia, Brazil, and Canada took in almost 15 million people.

So when you're trying to trace your family members from overseas, ask if any emigrated to other countries.

one last look at your homeland. As the ship pulls out of port, you stare at the ocean. It looks endless. You wonder: "Will I ever arrive in America? What will happen to me when I do?"

Of course, not all immigrants left for America in this fashion. Your family may have come by jet plane, and their stories may be filled with details of airline terminals and visa worries and quotas and 10-hour flights. Or they may have come by land—driving, walking, or riding across the Canadian or Mexican border.

If your ancestors arrived as slaves, or as poor people in the 1840s or 1850s, they may have come on "coffin ships"—boats so cramped and awful that the conditions above would have seemed luxurious by comparison.

For those who came willingly, one of the most painful moments was telling the people they loved that they might never see them again.

This was the case for Jade Snow Wong's father, who emigrated from Canton province, China, to San Francisco in 1903. "Many years later, when I was a grown woman, he told me with sadness that when he had asked his mother, whom he adored, for permission to come to the United States, she expressed her reluctance," Ms. Wong writes. When this only son insisted that he must leave, his mother scolded him: "Go! Go! You will have the life to go, but not the life to return!"

Making the decision to emigrate was only the first step. Most immigrants could not just leave for America the next day. Money had to be raised for the ticket; permits, passports, and visas had to be arranged; provisions

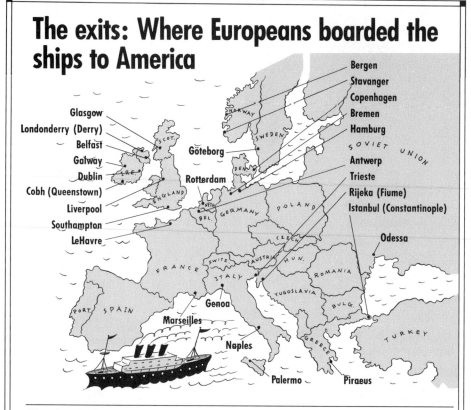

The exits: Where Europeans boarded the ships to America

Glasgow
Londonderry (Derry)
Belfast
Galway
Dublin
Cobh (Queenstown)
Liverpool
Southampton
LeHavre

Göteborg
Rotterdam
Genoa
Marseilles
Naples
Palermo

Bergen
Stavanger
Copenhagen
Bremen
Hamburg
Antwerp
Trieste
Rijeka (Fiume)
Istanbul (Constantinople)
Odessa
Piraeus

Most immigrants came to America by ship. Before they sailed, they had to get to a seaport that could accommodate giant ocean-going ships. Immigrants came from Asian cities like Canton, China, and slaves were brought in from West African ports. But most immigrants before 1965 came from Europe. On this map, you see the major ports from which Europeans left.

What they brought

An Italian immigrant family with its hands full. The pillowcase probably held pots.

Here is what some people remember carrying with them to America:

"My mother had her trunk just chock full of stuff, all our clothes, and a lot of food that my grandmother liked, all kinds of cheese . . . and sausage."
—Margaret Lehan, an Italian immigrant in 1911

"We brought candlesticks, of course, and a samovar [for making tea]. That was important. My mother brought shawls for some of the relatives here that they couldn't get—woolen shawls. Breakable things she packed into the bedding, and a couple of copper pans."
—Evelyn Golbe, a Russian Jewish immigrant in 1914

"I arrived in New York in 1921—all my belongings consisted of a change of underwear and two books."
—Abraham Burstein, a Russian Jewish immigrant in 1921

"I only had a suitcase with me. That's all I had."
—Josephine Marsanopoli, an Italian immigrant in 1921

"I didn't have a suitcase. . . . I had a little basket, like a trunk. I didn't have too many clothes to pack and I had some dolls that I had forever and ever."
—Irma Busch, a German immigrant in 1925

"Our clothes, our pillows, our big, thick comforters made from pure goose feathers—not chicken feathers. . . . And my mother made some cheese balls which could travel without refrigeration."
—Fannie Shock, a Polish immigrant in 1921

Doors to America:
Which one did your family come through?

During the 1980s, refugees from the Caribbean island of Haiti entered the United States through Miami, Florida. Many came in small, crowded boats like this one.

Where did your ancestors enter the United States? If you know the answer to that question, there's a good chance that you can find a copy of their records.

For a huge number of Americans, the answer is "Ellis Island"—it's estimated that more than one out of every three Americans can trace at least one ancestor back to there.

But more than 100 other U.S. cities and towns all over the country also served as an entry place for new Americans. And your ancestors could have come in through any of those. If you know where and approximately when they arrived, finding their records will be much easier.

For the first 300 years of immigration, most people arrived by boat. Besides New York—before, during, and after the Ellis Island years—a few other East Coast cities received a sizable number of immigrants. Boston was a major landing spot for Irish immigrants. Baltimore took in a substantial number of Germans. Philadelphia was another major port, a destination for many Italians and eastern Europeans.

In the 1800s, Charleston, South Carolina, and New Orleans, Louisiana, had busy years as immigrant ports. Galveston, Texas, was an unusual but important destination for thousands of immigrants from eastern Europe in the early 1900s. On the West Coast, San Francisco was the busiest boat arrival point, with most immigrants coming from Asia and the Pacific islands. Seattle and Los Angeles also received newcomers.

Not everyone came by boat, of course. Cities on the Mexican border—like El Paso, Texas, and Nogales, Arizona—have been entry points for millions of Mexicans and Latin Americans who walked, drove, or rode into the United States, particularly in the second half of this century. Up north, St. Albans, Vermont, and Detroit, Michigan, are among the checkpoints for those coming through Canada.

In some ways, immigration has changed a great deal over the past 25 years. If your family came to the United States since the 1960s, most of the paperwork (including the medical examination) was done in the country of origin. There's a good chance your family arrived by plane. The trip probably took hours, not days. And they could have entered the United States in any of a hundred airports.

There are, however, three major cities that attract most immigrants today.

The first is Miami, Florida. This tropical city on the Atlantic Ocean has become *the* major entryway for immigrants from South America and the Caribbean, and they have given Miami a new identity as an international city. More than half of all Miamians today

were born outside the United States!

New York is still probably the greatest entryway for foreigners coming to live in this country. Tens of thousands arrive from Europe, Asia, and South America every year. Many settle in the New York area and become U.S. citizens. In 1988, more than 40,000 immigrants took the oath to become a citizen in New York City.

But today another city appears ready to take over the reputation of the "Ellis Island of the 1990s": Los Angeles, California. Over the past 20 years, hundreds of thousands of immigrants have poured into Los Angeles. The greatest number come from Central America, especially Mexico. Many others are from the nations of Asia—Vietnam, Korea, the Philippines, and the Soviet Union. In the 1980s, more immigrants became citizens in Los Angeles—about 60,000 a year—than in any other city in the United States.

Japanese immigrants arriving in San Francisco in 1920. Until 1965, restrictive laws put severe limits on the number of Asians entering the United States.

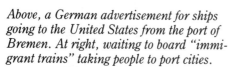

Above, a German advertisement for ships going to the United States from the port of Bremen. At right, waiting to board "immigrant trains" taking people to port cities.

had to be made for family members left behind.

Often fathers went to America first, worked to earn money, and then brought over their wives and children. Millions of immigrants, however, were single young men who came by themselves to earn a living. Some promised to bring over other family members when they raised enough money. Others intended to return to their homeland after making a fortune.

Children under 16 could not travel without their parents. Young women under 21 were not permitted to leave a country unless someone was waiting to meet them in America.

If an entire family was leaving, they probably sold just about everything they owned. Most immigrants took only what they could carry. They filled a trunk with clothing, bedsheets, pillows, some pieces of silverware, a framed photograph of the loved ones they left behind, and maybe a Bible or a set of candlesticks.

If there was room, women would wrap things like dishes and pots in the bedsheets. After all, these *would* be absolutely necessary in the New World. Men would often carry the tools of their trade: A barrel maker would bring along his special knife, for example. But families had to leave be-

hind furniture, most kitchenware, and probably most of their children's playthings (though a number of dolls and teddy bears did make the trip).

Many immigrants were afraid that they would never taste their favorite local foods again, so they stocked up for the trip. Greeks brought olives and figs. Eastern Europeans made sure to take their local sausages. Religious Jews brought kosher foods. Italians lugged bottles of wine, olive oil, fruits and nuts, and cheeses. "My mother . . . made a box full of Italian biscuits," recalled Pasquale Forlinghieri. "She figured [the food] would last at least for eight or nine days: 'If I don't like their food, I'm not going to go hungry.' "

When someone left a small town, it was a big and sometimes sad event. "Half of Polotzk was at my uncle's gate in the morning to conduct us to the railway station, and the other half was there before we arrived," remembered Mary Antin, who left Russia in 1893. "The procession resembled both a funeral and a triumph. The women wept over us, reminding us eloquently of the perils of the sea, the bewilderment of a foreign land, and the torments of homesickness that awaited us. . . .

"The last I saw of Polotzk was a . . . mass of people, waving colored hand-kerchiefs . . . falling on each other's necks, gone wild altogether. Then the station became invisible, and the shining tracks spun out from sky to sky. I was in the middle of the great, great world, and the longest road was mine."

Aboard Ship

When the immigrants arrived at the departure seaport, they were examined by doctors, government officials, and steamship company officers before boarding ship. These inspections were used by the shipping companies to weed out those who were ill or ineligi-

ble to emigrate—because if a passenger was rejected in America, the company had to pay for his or her return trip to Europe.

For a lucky few—the wealthy—the trip would be a comfortable one. Steamships had fine first- and second-class cabin accommodations for those who could afford them.

But most immigrants traveled third class—in steerage. That meant they found themselves on the lowest deck with dozens, even hundreds of people and no assigned places. The next

Steerage passengers on the ship Westernland *come out onto their small deck for a few minutes of fresh air on the way to New York, 1901.*

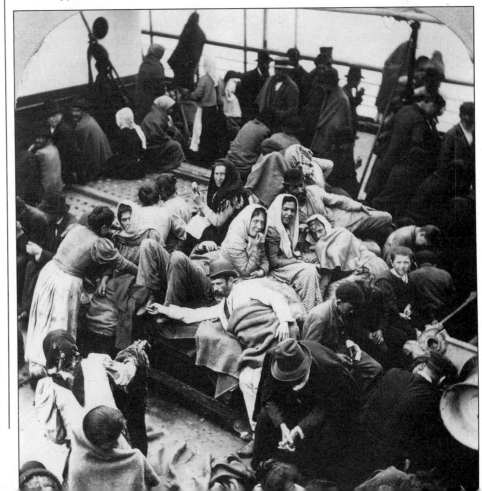

weeks were often very difficult. Conditions were unsanitary and many felt ill. Some passengers spent entire weeks in their beds.

"The boat was...terrible, horrible," said Josephine Reale, who came from Italy to Philadelphia in 1920 when she was only five and a half years old. "We were like cows, all bunched up together. Of course we were seasick and we hated the food....It was...terrible."

For some children, however, the steamer was a great new playground. "For 16 days the ship was our world," recalled Mary Antin. "I explored the ship, made friends with officers and crew, or pursued my thoughts in quiet nooks."

The long days and nights slowly wore down even the children's enthusiasm. All there was to see was the vast blue-green water. Then, just as the trip seemed to be lasting forever, someone would spot land.

"Oh joyful sight! We saw the tops of two trees!" remembered Mary Antin. "What a shout there rose! Everyone pointed out the welcome sight to ev-

Hats are lifted and passengers cheer as the Statue of Liberty comes into view in New York Harbor. Soon, these immigrants will arrive at Ellis Island.

eryone else, as if they did not see it. All eyes were fixed on it as if they saw a miracle. And this was only the beginning of the joys of the day!"

Soon, all the passengers would crowd onto the top deck. Arrival was drawing near—America was only a short time away! Finally, their lives could begin anew.

Arriving in America: What the Welcome Was Like

What your ancestors did when they first arrived in the United States depends on when and where they arrived.

In the very early days of immigration, newcomers faced no examinations and were given no guidance when their ships entered ports like New York, Boston, or New Orleans. Those who survived the trip on crowded, filthy ships were very happy to disembark. They were free to head out on their own.

Two groups, of course, were exceptions: Slaves were held until they were sold at auction; and indentured servants had to wait till they were assigned families.

Soon after the Revolutionary War, in the early 1800s, the new federal gov-

ernment started paying attention to how people entered this country. Congress was concerned about unhealthy conditions on board ships bringing immigrants, and about the people who died before they reached port. They were also worried that diseases were being brought into the United States.

In 1819, Congress passed the first law to improve conditions for immigrants. It limited the number of people a ship could carry, and required captains to compile a list of passengers, called a ship's manifest. If anyone died aboard ship, his or her name had to be recorded. These lists were held by the official in charge of the port.

For the next four decades, records were kept—though not very carefully—by the states. In just about every state from New York to Louisiana, doctors boarded ships to check for people with infectious diseases. Ill passengers were quarantined in hospitals, where they were supposed to be cured before setting foot in their new country.

As the flood of immigrants grew, it was obvious that a more organized system was needed. Finally, in 1855, the first official receiving station in the United States devoted solely to the processing of new immigrants was opened in New York City.

The station, called Castle Garden, had previously been a fort, an amusement hall, and an opera house. It was chosen because it could hold thousands of newcomers (10,000 people had jammed into it just a few years earlier to see the famous Swedish singer Jenny Lind).

For the next three decades, the state of New York ran Castle Garden as an overstuffed center for immigrant inspections. To Europeans, its name became a word—*Kassel gardena*—meaning "incredibly busy, noisy place." In this one great building, thousands of immigrants a day were inspected for disease, informed about jobs, and directed to their final destinations.

New York City was processing more than 7 of every 10 immigrants who arrived in the United States. Castle Garden—once thought to be so huge—was turning out to be too small. Then in 1875, the government passed the first of what would be many laws denying admission to certain groups of people. That meant inspectors had to spend more time examining arrivals. The need for a bigger building became crucial.

In 1890, a little island in New York Harbor just north of the Statue of Liberty was chosen as the location for a new processing center.

It was an unremarkable place, and over the years it had been known by a number of names: Gull Island, Oyster Island, Bucking Island, Gibbet Island. Soon, however, it would become one of the most famous—and feared—places in the world.

It was called Ellis Island.

Castle Garden, the first official American immigrant processing center.

New arrivals, many of them holding their identification tags between their teeth, step off a ferryboat and onto Ellis Island.

The Isle of Hope and Tears

On January 1, 1892, a 15-year-old Irish girl named Annie Moore walked off a ferryboat and into history, becoming the first person ever processed at the new immigration station on Ellis Island.

Annie and her two younger brothers arrived in New York on the steamship *Nevada* to join their parents, who had come to New York in 1888. Federal officials presented her with a 10-dollar gold piece as a symbol of the great moment. Annie "had never seen a

United States coin, and this was the largest sum of money she had ever possessed," *The New York Times* reported the next day.

The station had opened just as the greatest wave of immigration in world history was about to begin. Over the next 30 years, nearly 20 million people, most of them from southern and eastern Europe, entered the United States.

To the 12 million immigrants who would follow in Annie's footsteps on Ellis Island during that time, the processing center was far more than just a place where people were examined and their papers filled out. It was a place where lives were changed forever. Were you fit to be an American? Should you be allowed through the "Golden Door"? Was your life about to begin anew—or were you going to be sent back to the Old Country? These questions hung in the air for each immigrant as his steamship came into New York Harbor. Was that little island just beyond the Statue of Liberty the beginning—or the end—of a dream?

Ellis Island had not been built for everyone, however. Few rich passengers (those who traveled to America in

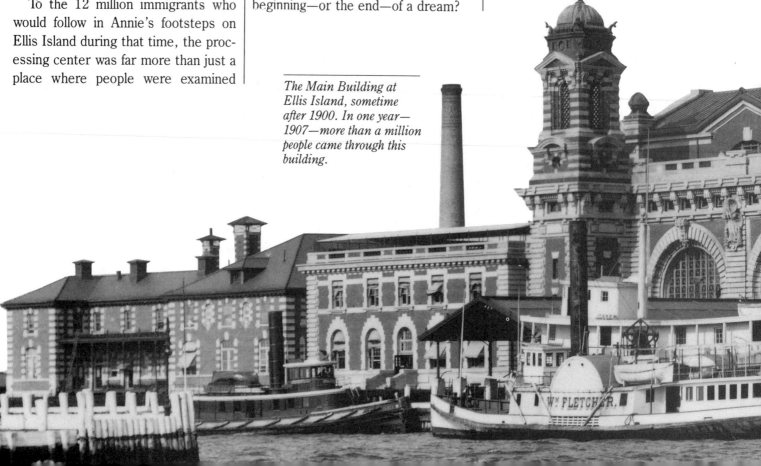

The Main Building at Ellis Island, sometime after 1900. In one year— 1907—more than a million people came through this building.

first- or second-class cabins) ever set foot on the island. It was for the steerage passengers that Ellis lay in wait.

Where the Immigrants Were Processed

When Annie Moore arrived in 1892, all the buildings on Ellis Island were made of wood. There was a small hospital, a baggage area, a restaurant, a dormitory, and a power station. The biggest structure of all was the three-story-tall reception building, with four peaked towers at its corners. This building must have appeared immense to the immigrants—more than 5,000 people could pass through it at once.

For five years, these wooden buildings were filled with the sounds of nervous immigrants. Then around midnight on June 14, 1897, a fire broke out and quickly burned the entire station to the ground. No one died in the fire, but most of the records of those who had arrived in this country since 1855 disappeared with the buildings.

Because Ellis Island had become so important, the U.S. Congress immedi-

They made it! These immigrants passed their tests on Ellis Island and have been admitted to the United States. Next stop: their new homes in America.

ately set aside money for a new set of buildings to be constructed. These buildings were to be fireproof, made of stone and concrete. During the two and a half years it took to build the new processing center, all immigrants to New York were processed at the tiny Barge Office on nearby Manhattan Island.

Finally, on December 17, 1900, Ellis Island reopened. Its handsome new buildings were made of red brick trimmed with white limestone. There was a hospital, a post office, a customs house, a power house, staff housing, and offices.

Grandest of all was the Main Building. It was three stories tall in its center section, with two large, two-story side pavilions. Four 100-foot-high towers, topped by copper domes that ended in sky-reaching spires, stood at the corners of its center section. At the main entrance, three tall archways guarded by stone eagles announced that this was a very important building.

The Long Arrival

The great steamships that brought the immigrants to America did not land at Ellis, however. In fact, the process of arrival in New York was a long one. For many immigrants, it must have been both exciting and frustrating.

These giant ocean liners, which carried as many as 2,000 passengers, sailed into New York Harbor through a narrow passageway, known as "The Narrows," between Long Island and Staten Island. Shortly after the steamship pulled through The Narrows, a little immigration tugboat would come alongside it.

On this small boat were officers of the U.S. Immigration Service. They came on board and met with the steamship officers. The immigration officials had two jobs to do. The first was to learn if any passenger had a disease that might spread to other people—illnesses like typhus, smallpox, or diphtheria.

"Have there been any cases of contagious disease on board?" an immigration officer would ask the ship's doctor.

"None at all," the doctor might respond.

In that case, the officials went on to their second job. They met with the immigrants in the expensive first- and second-class cabins, asking these "cabin" passengers a few questions and checking their passports. The

These immigrants may have caught a disease on the way to America. They were put aboard this ferry, then sent to a detention center until the threat of infection passed.

ship's doctor then gave the well-off immigrants a quick physical examination. If cabin passengers passed both exams, they were informed that they had been admitted to America without having to visit Ellis Island.

Occasionally, however, the ship's captain told the immigration officials, "Yes, we've discovered contagious disease among our passengers." In those cases, all passengers who might be infected were taken off ship and put into isolation. Those who were ill were sent to a hospital on Hoffman Island, a dot of land close to Staten Island; they would stay there until they recovered.

Passengers who had been exposed to the illness but had not come down with it were sent to nearby Swinburne Island. They were kept under observation in a clinic until it was certain that they had not caught the disease.

In most cases, the ship was free of contagious disease. Immigration officials finished their job and left, allowing the ship to complete the last leg of its long voyage.

Shortly after the cabin passenger inspections were over, the Statue of Liberty came into view. As the steerage passengers crowded on deck to get a look at the famous "Lady with the Lamp," few of them noticed that

The lamp beside the golden door

Lady Liberty in pieces, before she was assembled on Bedloe's Island (later Liberty Island) in New York Harbor.

Millions of foreigners will never forget the first American woman they met. She stood 151 feet tall, and wore a spiky crown and a long green robe. Beneath her feet were broken chains. In her right hand, thrust high into the sky, was a glowing torch. In her left hand was a book with the date "July 4, 1776" inscribed on its cover.

Their first view of her came as they crowded onto the deck of a ship entering New York Harbor. Many stood and silently stared. Some cheered. And more than a few cried when they looked up at this great symbol of freedom welcoming them to their new home.

The statue of "Liberty Enlightening the World" had been a gift to Americans from the French people, symbolizing the friendship between the two countries. Its cost was raised by contributions from the French, just as the cost of the pedestal on which it stood was raised by American donations.

The statue was born at an 1865 dinner party. French professor and writer Edouard de Laboulaye, the host, talked about giving a monument that would celebrate American liberty and promote support for democracy in France. Sculptor Frédéric Auguste Bartholdi, a guest at the party, was excited by the concept—and for the next 20 years, he worked on it. Bartholdi visited the United States in 1871 and saw the site for the great statue—tiny Bedloc's Island, which is now known as Liberty Island, in the heart of New York Harbor.

Fund-raising in France began in 1875. At first, Bartholdi wanted the statue ready for the American republic's 100th anniversary in 1876. He was only able to finish the arm and the torch by that time, so those pieces were sent to Philadelphia for the celebration.

The arm and torch were transferred to a park in New York City in 1877. They remained there for eight years, a reminder to Americans that *we* had to raise money for the pedestal.

The statue was completed in 1884. A year later, it was taken apart, placed in 214 boxes, sent on the steamship *Isère* to New York, and stored on Bedloe's Island until the pedestal was completed. Finally, with money raised by millions of contributors—including

The Statue has lifted her lamp to greet immigrants since 1886. In the background, the coast of New Jersey.

American schoolchildren who donated pennies and nickels—the pedestal was finished and the statue raised. It was unveiled at a huge dedication ceremony on October 28, 1886.

At the time, little was said about a poem called "The New Colossus," written three years earlier to help raise funds for the pedestal. The author, a young Russian Jewish woman named Emma Lazarus, was not even invited to the dedication ceremony. In her poem, Lazarus called the statue "Mother of Exiles," and focused not on the abstract idea of "freedom," but on the people coming to win that freedom. Lazarus's words have become world famous:

Give me your tired, your poor,
Your huddled masses yearning to
    breathe free,
The wretched refuse of your teeming
    shore,
Send these, the homeless, tempest-
    tost to me,
I lift my lamp beside the golden door!

In 1903, Emma Lazarus's poem was placed on a plaque and attached, permanently, to the Statue of Liberty's base.

Beware of swindlers!

Polish immigrant Stanislaus Plzybis-chewski was a very happy young man in May 1913. He was 22 years old. He had just been accepted into the United States as an immigrant. And he had a $50 bill in his pocket.

As Stanislaus walked down the paths of Ellis Island on his way to the ferry that would take him to Manhattan, he must have been very excited.

Suddenly, a red-faced man in a uniform stopped him in the hallway.

"What kind of money do you have?" the official asked.

The Polish boy showed his $50 bill.

"That money is no good," the man told him in German. He took the $50 bill and handed the boy a coin with a hold in the middle.

"Take this instead," the man said, then disappeared.

Stanislaus stood for a moment, confused. Then he realized what had happened: He'd been swindled.

The coin he held was from Argentina, and it was worth about four cents.

This story is one of hundreds told about how immigrants were cheated soon after arrival. Smooth talkers and con artists often gathered near immigration stations, waiting for a newcomer to wander by. These crooks knew that immigrants were dazed and confused by their long trip, and unfamiliar with American ways.

Some pretended to be relatives of the immigrants. "Hello, I was sent for you. Let me carry your bag," one might say. Two seconds later, the crook would disappear with the bag.

Others dressed as officials. In Stanislaus's case, the immigration officials on Ellis Island helped him look for the swindler, but they could not find him. "Men come to the island with caps and uniform jackets in their pockets, and it's hard to keep them out," one of the officials explained when asked how such a terrible thing could have happened.

Sometimes, immigrants were cheated by the very people they were supposed to trust, including immigration officials, money-changers, and restaurant help.

The U.S. government did try in a number of ways to protect the new immigrants from swindles. Investigations were held and inspectors were hired. Most people got through the process without being hoodwinked. But there were a number of immigrants who had to learn the hard way that America was a land of opportunity—for crooks as well as for everyone else.

just a few hundred yards beyond the statue were the red brick buildings of Ellis Island. This was where the steerage passengers would undergo *their* immigration processing.

Finally, the ship pulled into its final destination, a pier on the New York or New Jersey coastline. The wealthy passengers would leave, free to start their new lives. Steerage passengers, meanwhile, remained on board. Eventually, they were brought off the ship, lined up, divided into small groups, and then led to a ferry or barge. Hundreds of them, all carrying their luggage, were crowded onto the boats. They were taken to Ellis Island and quickly led into the Main Building.

Inside the Main Building

Inside that imposing building were many rooms, large and small. The immigrants' first stop was the baggage room on the ground floor, where they were expected to leave their luggage. Up the stairs were the immigration offices, a cafeteria, a place to exchange foreign money for American dollars, and a railroad ticket office. Also on this floor were the galleries where medical examinations and mental tests would be given.

At the center of the building was the greatest space of all—the Registry Room, better known as the Great Hall. This huge space, more than 50 feet high and filled with light and noise, was a place millions of immigrants would never forget.

It had a wraparound balcony looking down on the main floor. Light streamed through enormous windows. New York City, with its fabled skyscrapers, was framed in some windows; in others, the Statue of Liberty loomed.

For the first 11 years it was open, the Great Hall looked like a maze. It

The Ellis Island maze: From 1900 till 1911, the Great Hall inside the Main Building was broken into tiny sections by a jumble of iron railings.

was divided into sections by railings, and confused immigrants were jammed in tightly as they waited their turn for processing. After 1911, the railings were taken down and rows of more comfortable benches were placed throughout the hall.

On the third floor of the Main Building were hearing rooms, where some immigrants were sent to appear before "Boards of Special Inquiry." A special inquiry was a kind of mini-trial, in which a group of inspectors asked a newcomer questions and determined whether or not he or she should be admitted. Many immigrants appeared before these boards; most of them were found acceptable.

If for any reason they were found ineligible to enter the United States—because of a physical handicap, illness, or because they did not strike the officer as someone likely to be able to support themselves in this country—they could be rejected and deported. This meant they would be held until the steamship they had arrived on could return them to the port from which they had come.

For the majority of immigrants, a visit to Ellis Island took no more than three or four hours. Most left happily—98 percent passed all inspec-

Answer a few questions, please

Immigrants spent anywhere from two hours to a day or more at the immigration center. A series of questions had been asked on the ship over, and now inspectors asked the same questions again to see if the answers matched. They asked questions like these:

1. What is your name?
2. How old are you?
3. Are you married or single?
4. What is your calling or occupation?
5. Are you able to read or write?
6. What is your nationality?
7. Where was your last residence?
8. Which U.S. seaport have you landed in?
9. What is your final destination in the United States?
10. Do you have a ticket to your final destination?
11. Did you pay for your passage over? If not, who did?
12. Do you have money with you? More than $30? How much? Less? How much?
13. Are you going to join a relative? What relative? Name and address?
14. Have you ever been to the United States before? Where and when?

An Italian immigrant waits his turn to answer an inspector's questions.

15. Have you ever been in prison, in a poorhouse, or supported by charity?
16. Are you a polygamist?
17. Are you under contract, expressed or implied, to perform labor in the United States?
18. What is the condition of your health, mental and physical?
19. Are you deformed or crippled? If so, by what cause?

tions and were sent on to their final destinations. A few were detained, some waiting for relatives to pick them up, others confined to the hospital until their infectious diseases were cured. Only 2 out of 100 arrivals were rejected and deported.

For millions, Ellis Island was only a stop on the way to a new home somewhere in America. Two out of every three Ellis Island immigrants left the New York area. They converted their foreign money to American dollars at the island's exchange, then bought a ticket at the Ellis Island railroad office.

Many took a ferry to New Jersey, where they caught trains chugging into the heartland of America. For some, this could be a short ride—a day, perhaps, to Pennsylvania or Maryland. For others, however, the train ride was

Some new arrivals entered the United States through Baltimore, Maryland. Many went directly from their ship to immigrant trains heading for the Midwest.

What is your final destination?

An immigrant has just passed inspection at Ellis Island. He wants to know how to reach the city where his brother is waiting. So he approaches an inspector and says, "Excuse me. I go Tseekago. Where for train?"

The inspector, if he is friendly and able to understand the immigrant's accent, may say, "Oh, you mean Chicago. Let me write it down for you."

But sometimes, inspectors had difficulty deciphering the places that immigrants pronounced or wrote down. In nearly every case, someone was able to figure out the correct answer. But a few times, the immigrants ended up far from where they wanted to go.

Where, for example, was "Pringvilliamas"? It took a clever inspector to figure out that it was Springfield, Massachusetts. Inspectors also had to decipher "Linkinbra" (Lincoln, Nebraska), "Neihork, Nugers" (Newark, New Jersey), and "Deas Moynes, Yova" (Des Moines, Iowa). And one bright immigration officer

was able to translate "Szekeneveno Pillsburs" into "Second Avenue, Pittsburgh."

What about "Settlevash"? Jeanette

Stirling, who came to the United States from Turkey in the early 1900s, took a train across the country on her way to her new home in Washington State. "When we got to Seattle," she remembered, "we were all sitting together, a lot of immigrants with their bundles. There was a committee that came to meet us. They said, 'Well, where are you going?'

"We said, 'We're going to Settlevash.'

"They said, 'Get off the train. This is Seattle, Washington.'

"And we said, 'No, we're going to Settlevash.' We wouldn't budge."

And there is the famous story about an immigrant who arrived at Ellis Island and wished to go to Houston. He was promptly put on a train to Texas. At some point, the big mistake was discovered; he really wanted to go to Houston *Street* on New York City's Lower East Side. Legend says that at least one immigrant became a cowboy instead of a tailor because of an inspector's mistake.

a long journey. Many Swedes and Norwegians headed for the Great Plains, Germans to Pennsylvania, Poles to the cities of the Midwest, Greeks or Spaniards to Washington State or Nevada. Others took the ferry to New York, where they caught trains to their final destinations in the Northeast or upstate New York.

But no matter how long they stayed there, everyone who stepped onto the "Isle of Tears"—as Ellis Island soon came to be known around the world because of the deportations and tearful family separations—remembered it. To many, it was one of the most frightening and awe-inspiring experiences of their lives.

A Day on the Island

Seventeen-year-old Jacob was one of 1,450 steerage passengers who arrived in New York Harbor on a cold day in December 1902. While first- and second-class cabin passengers headed for their new homes, Jacob and his steerage companions were led to a gangplank at the ship's rear. They walked onto a pier where one of the ship's officers called their names, mispronouncing many. The immigrants were then arranged in groups of 30.

Each group was made up of passen-

Slavic women at Ellis Island, around 1900. They have come to join their families in America. The cards hanging around the women's necks may be ship identification markers or railroad tickets.

gers whose names appeared on one page of the ship's manifest. The United States had strict rules about these lists; every page could have no more than 30 names. Jacob's name was on page 20, line 10, and he was gathered with all the other passengers listed on page 20.

Someone gave Jacob an identifica-

tion tag. "It's very important," he was told. "Don't lose it." The tag—with a big number 20 and a small number 10—was pinned to Jacob's black coat.

A ferry brought Jacob and his fellow passengers to Ellis Island. An inspector met the group and marched them quickly into the Main Building's baggage room. "You can leave your bags

Ellis was called the "Isle of Hope and Tears" because people didn't know if they'd be allowed to enter the United States till they got through all the inspections. At right, a group of children nervously wait with their mothers for special examinations. Below, a man who had been detained tries on a jacket in the clothing room. Next to him, the portrait of a proud Russian Cossack immigrant. And next to him, dozens of "greenhorns"—new arrivals who have been admitted—wait to exchange their foreign money for American dollars.

At right, dozens of immigrants sit down to a meal in the Ellis Island cafeteria. Josephine Reale, who was five when she arrived from Italy, remembers: "We were hungry…but we couldn't eat the bread. Our Italian bread was so delicious. We couldn't understand this soft, mushy bread. It had a horrible taste. I like it now, but in those days, we hated it! We thought, 'Oh dear God, is this the kind of bread we're going to have to eat in America?'" Below, immigrant boys being examined by a health officer, 1911. Below right, an immigrant from Denmark holds his cane and considers his future.

"Please don't send me back." Sometimes immigrants were pulled aside and sent to a hearing, called a Board of Special Inquiry. Inspectors listened to their stories and voted on whether to admit them or turn them away.

here," a translator told the immigrants—but Jacob's duffel bag contained everything he owned, and if someone stole it he'd be lost. He carried it with him the whole day. Many of his fellow passengers, Jacob noticed, did the same.

"Hurry up!" an inspector barked, pointing to a wide staircase. "Let's go." Jacob bounded up the steps quickly—not knowing that he and his fellow passengers were already being examined.

Government doctors stood at the top of the staircase, watching. Did anyone have a bad leg? Was someone out of breath? When Jacob arrived at the doctors' station, they looked over his hands, hair, neck, and face. Then a doctor asked through an interpreter: "Are you healthy? Do you have any rashes? Have you ever had tuberculosis?" Everything was in order; Jacob moved on down the line. But he noticed that the doctors took out a piece of chalk and wrote something on the coats of some immigrants.

These doctors were signaling other doctors that a newcomer appeared to have a problem. Each problem had a letter: "H" stood for possible heart condition; "L" meant lame; "B" indicated a back problem; "X" said the person seemed mentally slow. There was also "F" for rash on the face; "Ft" for foot problems; and "K" for hernia.

Anyone whose clothing had been marked was referred to a specialist for closer examination. Jacob and the rest of the group, meanwhile, moved to the next exam: the dreaded eye test. He'd been told that it was quick and painful, and that a bad result could be disastrous. The doctor tilted the immigrant's head back and, with a hook used to button up old-fashioned gloves, pulled ever so slightly on his upper eyelids, looking for any sign of eye disease. If there was a problem, the doctor's chalk came out. If the problem was trachoma (an infectious disease that could be spread easily) he marked "CT" on the coat. Even though trachoma was very common, and a cure was eventually discovered, all people with "CT" on their coats were sent back home.

While the examinations were being conducted, Jacob suddenly realized he was in an extraordinary room, the Great Hall.

The hall was noisy and crowded, teeming with thousands of people—more than lived in all of Jacob's village! And they came from all over the world. Some wore their national costumes: Dutch people with wooden shoes or peaked hats, eastern European women wearing kerchiefs on their heads, Cossacks with long boots and fur hats. Their languages mixed together—Italian, Czech, Dutch, Russian, Polish, Hungarian, English, Yiddish, Spanish, and many more.

The last examination was by a government inspector. One by one, immigrants' names and their numbers on the ship's passenger list were called. Jacob stepped up to the table with an interpreter by his side. "What is your name? Where are you going? How much money do you have? Show it to me. Do you have a job already? Where

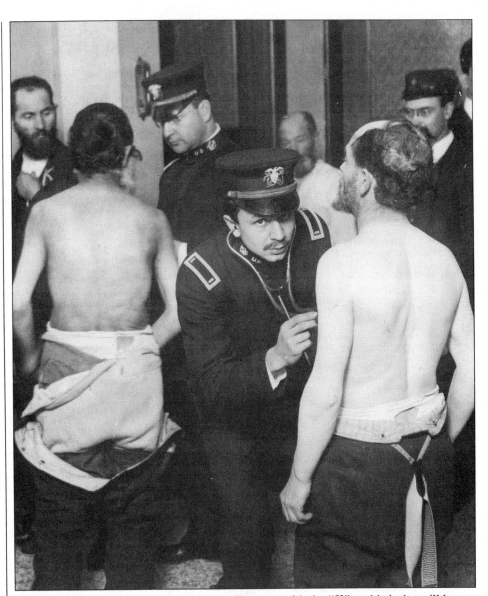

Ellis Island doctors examine immigrants. The man with the "K" on his jacket will be checked for a hernia.

The new Ellis Island Immigration Museum: At left, a view of the restored Great Hall. Below, a man looks for the name of one of his ancestors on the museum's Wall of Honor.

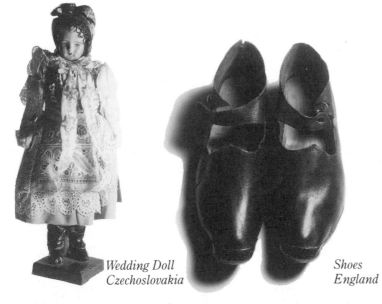

Wedding Doll
Czechoslovakia

Shoes
England

Rattle
Spain

Shoemaker's Last
Sweden

Packet of Medicine
Japan

Above, some of the many special items
donated to the museum by immigrants
and their families. At left, a sample of
the exhibits at the museum.

will you live? Whom are you coming to see?" The questions came rapidly. As he spoke, the inspector looked at page 20, line 10, matching Jacob's answers with what he had said when he boarded the ship. If any answer was suspect, the inspector might put a chalk mark "SI" on the immigrant's back and on the list. That stood for "Board of Special Inquiry," and meant this person had to attend a hearing to determine if he could be admitted.

A group of immigrants from southern Italy stares at the camera as they prepare for processing at Ellis Island.

A ferry loaded with immigrants who have passed Ellis Island tests heads for New York City. This boat landed in Manhattan near the old Castle Garden building.

Every minute of this last exam must have felt like forever for the nervous immigrants. Finally, the inspector nodded. For Jacob, America was just minutes away.

"Welcome to the United States," said the translator—and for the first time all day, Jacob broke into a huge smile.

"Where do I go?" he asked.

"There," the man pointed. "And good luck!"

Jacob walked through a door and out of the Great Hall. He was now in a small corridor where people were exchanging money and buying and selling food and train tickets to other parts of the United States. Jacob exchanged a little bit of money and bought a sandwich. He stared at a strange yellow fruit called a "banana," but he was afraid to buy it.

He then walked out the door to take the ferry to New York City. In the distance, he stared at the towering buildings. Could they be real?

As he approached the ferry station, Jacob spotted his uncle Abraham. They had not seen each other since Abraham had left for America five years before.

"Uncle Abe!" Jacob shouted.

"Jacob?" his uncle responded. "Is it really you, all grown up?"

The two hugged. Soon they boarded the ferry to downtown Manhattan, then began the trek to the East New York section in Brooklyn, where Jacob would live with his uncle.

Now, it was up to him to make what he could of himself. His new life had begun.

Coming over the border: Neighbors who immigrated

Most immigrants over the past 300 years have come to America by boat and have gone through immigration procedures in cities like New York and San Francisco. Some immigrants, however, entered the United States by land. They came from Canada and Mexico, and *their* arrivals were quite different.

For one thing, leaving home was not as difficult for Mexicans and Canadians as it was for Europeans and Asians. The trip was simpler, cheaper, and shorter; and if things did not work out, they could go home far more easily.

The whole immigration process was also less formal on land. There were no giant immigration centers as there were for boat arrivals. Much of the processing was done quickly at the border. And in fact, millions of people probably immigrated without any processing at all.

Hundreds of thousands have come to the United States from Mexico. In the 1920s, when the flow of immigrants from Europe was stopped by American law, Mexican workers were in great demand. U.S. railroad companies needed them to lay down tracks across the Southwest.

Many Mexicans came into the United States legally. Others sneaked across the border. They waded through shallow parts of the Rio Grande or hid in the trunks of cars driven in legally.

Today, Hispanic-Americans are the largest immigrant group in the nation. Hundreds of thousands of Mexican-Americans live in California, Texas, Arizona, and New Mexico.

There is also a great deal of new immigration from Mexico—legal and illegal, temporary and permanent. The U.S. government attempts to crack down on illegal immigration, but as long

This Mexican man was caught trying to enter the United States illegally in 1954 by an American immigration officer.

as Mexico and the nations of Central America remain poorer than the United States, there will probably be more people who wish to come here than the law allows.

Our northern neighbor, Canada, is richer and has far fewer people than Mexico. It is also a country to which many European immigrants came during the busiest years of immigration to the United States.

Some Canadians came to the United States because of economic problems in their country. Many were French-speaking residents of Quebec province, who have come since the 1850s to work in the mills, stone quarries, and lumber industries of the midwestern and New England states.

Other Canadians were actually Europeans who had first immigrated to Canada in the hopes that they would find it easier to be admitted into the United States. Some were then able to enter the United States; others were denied and had to remain in Canada.

Immigration works the other way, too. Over the years, a number of Americans have left the United States to live in Canada. Today, Canada and the United States still exchange citizens, and they are two of the most welcoming nations in the world for immigrants from everywhere.

Cars coming from Canada are inspected as they enter the United States.

CHAPTER FIVE

Exploring the Past

A STEP-BY-STEP GUIDE TO YOUR GENEALOGICAL TREASURE HUNT

I f you're asking yourself, "Where does *my* family fit in? Where and when did *we* enter America? What are the stories and legends of my ancestors?" then you're ready to begin the real work—and real fun—of genealogy. Remember those blank spaces on your Pedigree Chart? Now you have to try to fill them in. That means it's time for one of the biggest challenges for an Ancestor Detector: the genealogical treasure hunt.

You're not looking for coins or jewels, but for something just as precious—information that reveals something about your family, past or present. It might be a document with information about a long-lost relative,

or a ragged old sweater, or a piece of woodwork created by an ancestor. It might even be a memory or a story, funny or scary or wonderful, about someone in your family. Anything that mattered to one of your relatives is worth seeking out and studying for clues about an ancestor. The three best places to look for items that might supply information are family collections, official records and documents, and relatives' memories.

Here are tips on how to make the most of these sources.

Finding Family Collections

Information about your family is lurking in all kinds of places: family Bibles, baby books, photo albums, old papers and documents, citizenship papers, school records. Ask your parents and other relatives if they have any of these, and if you can look through them.

Many of these "treasures" may be old and in *very fragile* condition. Handle them with great care. Don't touch photographs, except on the edges. Handle old books very gently; their pages may crack or the spines may break if you are too rough with them.

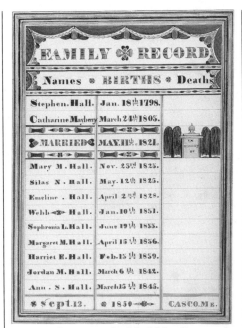

Discovering a wonderful old family record like this document from Maine would make a genealogist jump for joy.

Look at the front inside cover and the last pages. There may be an inscription or notes made by the previous owners. If the owners of these things are nervous about your examination, suggest that they turn the pages or handle the items while you just look. Write down any significant dates you find on your Family Group Sheets, noting where you found the information.

If you find an old family Bible, inspect the inside front and back covers,

Genealogical jewels

Here's a list of locations where family papers and treasures may be found. Ask your relatives if they have any of these items, and if you could see them.

Photo albums
Scrapbooks
Family Bibles
Bundles of letters
Baby books
Diaries
Old family recipe books
Other old books
School yearbooks, autograph books
Certificates (birth, christening, bar mitzvah, confirmation, school, military, marriage, divorce, death)
Deeds and wills
Announcements and invitations
Newspaper clippings
Identification cards
Trophies, plaques, or other awards
Inherited items (quilts, jewelry, books, candlesticks, furniture)
Charts or family trees
A family history

The family Bible

Once, nearly every family had its own "family records center," but it wasn't computerized, fancy, or expensive. It was a copy of the family Bible, the one book almost every home was sure to have. Within the pages of a King James Bible or an Old Testament (sometimes called a Chumash in Jewish families), someone in the family wrote down the names and dates of important events. This was the practice in millions of families, and not just in the United States.

Some Bibles came with spaces already provided for birth, marriage, and death dates. Other times, owners just wrote on blank pages. If your family has any Bibles that have been handed down, look them over carefully. Check the inside covers and the pages between the Old and New Testaments, which were the most common spots for registering information.

The most valuable Bibles are those that were kept as running records of family history. Some were passed down from parent to child, from generation to generation. If you come across an old Bible, ask yourself:

• Are the dates all written in the same

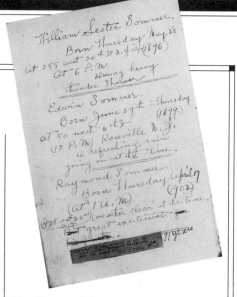

Family records in a family Bible.

handwriting?

• Is the color of the ink always the same, even for different dates?

If both answers are yes, your Bible may be a summary rather than an ongoing record. Often, family members copied dates from one source to another. If you suspect this is so, check the front of the Bible for a date of publication. If that date is after any of the births, you're looking at a summary.

But if the dates seem to have been written *as they occurred*, you may have found a special and accurate record of your family's vital events. Make a note of all information, being sure to indicate whether it came from an original record or from a summary.

and the exact middle of the book. Years ago, Bibles were often used to record the dates of family births, marriages, and deaths.

Citizenship papers, passports, old drivers' licenses, and school records often include a person's date and place of birth. They may also list the names of both parents (including the hard-to-find grandmother's maiden name).

Family photo albums can be wonderful resources. You may hear stories about the circumstances under which a photo was taken, or about the people in the picture. Just seeing photos of ancestors sometimes jogs peoples' memories, and may bring to mind a long-lost name.

Ask your relatives to talk about the people in the pictures. After they've identified who's who, you may want to ask them about the way people are dressed. Before about 1920, taking pictures was considered a great occasion and people often wore their best outfits. What were your ancestors wearing? What do the clothes say about them? Are they serious or lively, worn or new, dressy or everyday?

Where was each photograph taken? Check to see if the name of the photographer's studio, its location, or a date is on the back. Was the photograph taken near where your family lived, or was the studio far away?

If there is more than one person in the photograph, are the people related? Is everyone dressed the same way? Are their hairstyles the same? Are the women wearing head scarves and aprons and are the men wearing hats? If so, are they in the style of America or the Old Country?

The most precious articles in your family may not be rare or expensive, but rather those handed down from one generation to another, from father or mother to son or daughter. These items, called "heirlooms," are special mainly because of their history, and they are highly valued simply because they are beautiful or because they played a part in a family's past. Be on the lookout for them.

Old samplers (decorative pictures sewn onto cloth) or quilts that have been in the family for a long time may have names and dates of birth embroidered onto them.

Gently look underneath and behind pieces of furniture. Ask if you can look at the backs of paintings. Sometimes you may find notes or inscriptions on these, too.

Perhaps you will come across a clock that your great-grandfather

The author of this book could not make the wedding pictured above; his parents were getting married. But a few years later, he did manage to pose for the portrait at right.

made. Does anyone know when great-grandpa made it, or why? Did he make others? How did the person who owns it today receive it? Is there a story behind it?

You may find hundreds of other fascinating items in family collections: crocheted tablecloths or handmade dolls, a hat with a funny history, a portrait of a parent left behind in an-

Handling old family photographs

Photographs are not merely pieces of paper. They are chemical compositions, usually coated with gelatin and silver. Photos can be harmed by light, air, or dust. For that reason, they need to be protected.

• When you look at old photographs, handle them with great care. Be sure your hands are clean, and touch only the corners. Oil or dirt from fingers can ruin photos.

• Keep old photos out of temperature extremes. Don't store them in an attic or basement where it's hot or damp.

• If you can identify the photos in any way, it is a good idea to label them on the back. But never write with a ballpoint pen. Instead, use a Stabilo art pencil, which you can pick up in any art supply store for about $1. These pencils leave less of an impression than regular pencils. When you write, be sure not to press hard, and don't write on the area where people's faces are.

Another possibility is to buy gummed labels and write the information on them, again using a stabilo. Then you can carefully transfer the label to the back of the photo.

• Do not store photos one on top of the other. This is especially important if anything has been written on the back; ink can come off and ruin your pictures. Place acid-free paper between old photographs.

• Never fix an old photograph with cellophane tape; it cracks and will leave a residue. Also, don't attach photos with paper clips, bunch them together with rubber bands, or glue them into books.

other country, a book brought across the sea by a young woman who loved to read.

Be sure to enter any information you find out in your notebook. This could be as simple as writing a line or two on your great-uncle's Family Group Sheet about the trumpet he played in order to smuggle it past border guards. Or you could start a special Treasure Sheet, a page in your notebook filled with your impressions of what you saw. Write down the name of the person who showed the treasure to you, and where and when you saw it. You *must* keep track of where every bit of data comes from, because you may learn or discover conflicting information later. Knowing its source will help you decide what information is trustworthy.

Tracking Down Official Records and Documents

Amazingly, hundreds of official documents that contain information about your family do exist. They include vital records (birth, marriage, and death certificates), military records, citizenship papers, and ships' manifests.

You will probably find some of these documents in the homes of your relatives. For others, you may have to write or visit a records center. We'll take a close look at these records and how to use them in Chapter 8. For now, just remember to record every bit of information you find, including the number of the document (it may come in handy later), and double-check to be sure you don't make any errors. You might even ask for a photocopy of a document, if possible.

Relatives' Memories/Oral Histories

Memories are the most precious of all family treasures. Nothing can capture the essence of your family the way your grandparents and other relatives can. They have lived through some great events, and can recall them for you first-hand. They may remember the smallest details of significant family moments that aren't recorded any-

Old passports may include photos of your ancestors; this Greek passport dates from 1916.

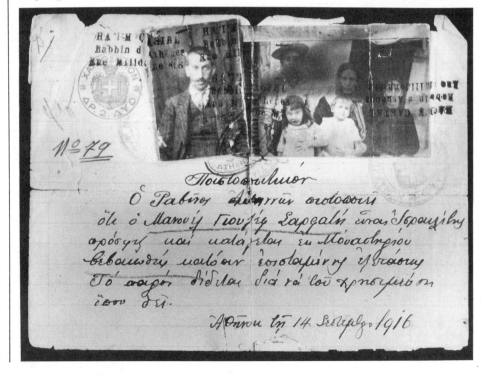

One of the best ways to fill in gaps in your family history is to talk with your relatives. If you can, bring along a tape recorder.

days of your family. They are, in fact, a precious link to the past. Someone born in 1920 can not only give you clear memories of the 1930s, but he or she may have heard first-hand tales of the 1880s from someone who was 70 years old in 1930. You may connect 100 years in one conversation!

But you won't always be able to sit down with your subjects. Some of them may live far away from you. In those cases, your interviews can take place over the telephone or by letter-questionnaire.

However you do it, conducting a successful oral history interview isn't always easy. Some of it depends on your relatives: what they know, what they are willing to talk about, and how much they remember.

But much depends on you and your ability to combine the best attributes of friend, hard-nosed reporter, and sensitive psychologist.

Thirteen Tips for a Successful Interview

In normal conversation, both people talk. Ideas are exchanged. Each person contributes information. The talk flows in unpredictable ways.

Interviews are a little different. One

where else. And these stories can bring ancestors to life.

When these spoken recollections are gathered, organized, and preserved, the information is called an "oral history." Oral histories do not grow out of rambling reminiscences— they are collected through carefully directed interviews. That's where you come in. As an Ancestor Detector, you get to ask the questions.

Whom do you think you should interview? Most genealogists would say,

"Everyone in the family." After all, probably every family member knows something no one else knows. And one of those memories may help you solve a piece of your family puzzle.

The best place to start is with the people you feel most comfortable with. Begin by interviewing your mom or dad, then move on to other relatives you know well. When you feel like you are an experienced interviewer, you'll want to talk with your oldest relatives. They know the most about the earliest person has a goal. You want to obtain information from another person (let's call him or her "the talker"). You want the talker to feel comfortable, but you need to direct the conversation to the points you are interested in.

You also have to be flexible. Sometimes an unexpected topic can turn out to be wonderful. Other times, you'll need to lead your talker back to the main point—without hurting his or her feelings. This can be difficult, but you will become better at it as you go along—practice will make you skilled. Be patient with yourself and expect some mistakes. To make things easier, keep these tips in mind:

1. Before you interview anyone, give advance warning. Explain what you want to do, why you want to do it, and why this person is important to you and your research. Here's one approach:

Dear Aunt Jesse:

I'm working on a history of our family, and it would be very helpful if I could sit down and talk with you. I'm particularly interested in your memories of my great-grandparents (your mother and father) and the family's early years in Minnesota.

I'd also love to look at any old photo-graphs or documents you have from the early days.

I won't need much more than an hour of your time, and would like to hold our talk at your home. Any weekend day would be fine. Can you let me know a date that is convenient for you?

Thanks so much for your help.

By writing this letter, you've given your relative a chance to start thinking about the topics you're interested in, and you may have even jogged her memory. Of course, not all your relatives will be close by, and your arrangements may be more difficult than "any weekend day." That just makes your writing—and planning—even more important.

2. Prepare before your interview. Find out whatever you can about this relative *before* the interview. Where

---

Tape recorder techniques

Tape or video recorders can be invaluable for documenting a family history. If you possibly can, bring a recorder to every interview.

Some people may feel a little self-conscious talking with a recorder on. Small tape recorders ease this problem; they are usually forgotten after a short period of time. Camcorders, on the other hand, are more intrusive and often require a second person to operate them.

Whichever recording device you use, it's a good idea to engage in small talk before you turn the recorder on, just to make the person feel comfortable. Then ease gently into the interview—with the recorder on. Ask

straightforward questions, like "How long have you lived here?" or "Can you tell me a little bit about this photograph? When was it taken? Who are the people in it?"

Before you begin, write the name, date, time, and place of the interview on the outside of the tape. Also speak those words into the recorder, so that this is the first thing you hear when you play the tape back: "Interview by Billy Jones with Aunt Jesse James, December 14, 1989, at her home on Collins Avenue in Miami, Florida, 2:30 Saturday afternoon."

When you end the interview, record this same information all over again.

The author's great-grandfather, who helped his son Max emigrate from Lomza, Poland.

does she fit into the family? What documents might she have? What other genealogical jewels might she have? (It's a good idea to send her a copy of the list on page 77 before you go.)

Whom did she meet that no one else knew, or whom might she remember best? Where did she live? Gather as much information as you can ahead of time about her relationship to everyone in your family. Your parents can probably help you with this.

3. Think out your questions beforehand. Interviewing requires structure. Write your questions on a sheet of paper, organized by subject. One easy way to organize what you want to ask is by years: Start with your relative's earliest years, and then move on from there.

"So, Aunt Jesse, you lived in the house outside Minneapolis till you were 10—about 1922, right? Then where did you move?" Or: "You say grandpa worked as a tailor in St. Paul. Did you ever visit his shop? Where was it? What years did he have the business there?"

As this interviewer did, it's a good idea to summarize what you already know so that your subject can verify your facts. Then move on to a request for more detail.

Sometimes the simplest questions can hit the jackpot. I asked my great-uncle Max, "How old were you when you went from Poland to America?" I didn't get an answer; I got a story:

"I must have been about 15 when I went to Warsaw to get a visa to emigrate. I got the visa, but then the counselor at the examination said, 'Listen, boy, you are underage. You can't go without your father.' He crossed out my stamp.

"I went back to our town and told my father. He said, 'Don't worry, we'll take care of that.'

"My father was a religious man, but he also knew how to get things done. He called a policeman from our town and asked him to make me older.

"I got new papers. Now I turned from 15 to 18 or 19. I went back to Warsaw, and I was able to leave. And on February 20, 1920, I took the boat *Siskehana* from Danzig to New York."

Remember to also ask open-ended questions. "What do you remember most about the apartment on Division Street?" or "Tell me about your relationship with your brothers" may yield something unexpected and wonderful.

4. If at all possible, bring a tape recorder. A small recorder usually doesn't disturb anyone, and it catches every bit of information, including the way your talkers sound and exactly how they answer questions. If you don't have a tape recorder, ask your parents if you can borrow or even rent one. (See "Tape Recorder Techniques" on page 83 for some suggestions.)

5. In any case, bring a notebook and pen. Even if you have a tape recorder, *always* take handwritten notes. Recorders have been known to break down.

During the interview, write down names and dates, and double-check them with your subject. Facts are important, but the most important information your talkers offer are their stories. Try to capture the way they talk, and their colorful expressions: "That ship was rolling on the ocean like a marble in your hand."

There's another good reason to bring pen and paper with you. You won't have to interrupt when you think of a question; just write a note to yourself so you'll remember to ask it at an appropriate time.

6. Start with easy, friendly questions. Leave the more difficult or emotional material for later in the interview, after you've had time to gain your talker's trust. If things aren't going well, you may want to save those questions for another time.

It's also a good idea to begin with questions about the person you're interviewing. You may be most interested in a great-grandfather if he is the missing link in your Pedigree Chart. But first get some background information about your talker—your aunt, for example. This serves two purposes. First, it lets her know she's important to you and that you care about her; second, it may reveal some other information you'd never have known about otherwise.

Also, when asking for dates, relate them to your talker. "How old were

The bustling marketplace in the Polish village of Lomza in the early 1900s.

Saving your own life

One of the best ways to practice putting together the story of your ancestors is by telling your own story. You may not think you have much to tell, but you do. Think of someone 100 years from now, wondering about your life. Imagine the questions he or she will have: Who were you? Where did you come from? What was your life like? What did you do with your days? What kind of home did you live in? Who else was in your family? What contact did you have with the other members of your family? Where had you traveled? What mattered most to you? What did you hope to accomplish?

You don't have to answer those particular questions. There may be others that are more important to you, that give more of a sense of who you are.

You choose.

Then sit down and try to write about yourself— something that will tell your descendants 100 years from now what it felt like, and was like, to be you.

You can use more than just words in this life history. Photographs are very helpful. So are relevant documents. There are dozens of possibilities here, in fact: your birth or baptismal certificate; a report card; an award for athletic or academic achievement; your medical or dental records; a map you draw of your neighborhood; letters you wrote, or letters someone wrote to you; a list of your favorite books, sports teams, movies, or records.

Describe what you look like: how tall

you are; what color your hair and eyes are; what kind of clothes you like to wear. Include whether you're quiet or outgoing, optimistic or pessimistic, energetic or slower-moving.

List your friends and the things you do for fun; what you do with your family; where your family has lived. You can list addresses, and maybe even describe what you remember about each home.

Be sure to include stories about yourself. Don't just tell what *you* remember; think about things you've heard about yourself from members of your family. Talk about things you're proud of, and things you've done that you're not so proud of. A little bit of the less-than-perfect side of your life will make your history much more honest and realistic.

Try to give a picture of day-to-day life. What does an apple cost? A bicycle? A new car? How much is a meal in a restaurant? What kinds of foods do you eat? How many hours a week do you go to school or work? How much free time do the people in your family have? Do your parents work outside the home? What do they do? About how much money do they make?

Talk about customs and rituals in your life. How you celebrate birthdays and holidays. What you do on weekends. If you are religious, and if so, how you practice your religion.

You will also want to give your future relatives a sense of the larger world you live in. What is life like in the 1990s in your family, in your town, in your state, and in your country? Maybe you should include a front page of a local newspaper, a copy of a news magazine, or a list of stories covered on the national TV news one night. Did any of those big news stories affect you? Explain how.

Once you've finished the report, date it. Then put it away somewhere safe. This document is going to be very valuable to you for a couple of reasons.

First of all, it will be a model to use when you write about your relatives. See if you can describe their personalities, their day-to-day lives, and the flavor of their times in the same spirit with which you captured your own.

Second, this report will be a wonderful record for you of this moment in time. Years from now, you will find it fun to reread and see who you were when you wrote it. In fact, you may want to write a new one every few years.

you when Uncle Bill died?" is often a better way of discovering when the event happened than simply asking, "What year did Uncle Bill die?"

7. Bring family photographs with you, and use them during the interview. Look for photos, artwork, or documents that will help jog your subject's memory. Bring the pictures out and ask your talker to describe what's going on. "Do you remember when this was taken? Who are the people? What was the occasion? Who do you think took the picture?" You may be amazed at how much detail Aunt Jesse will see in a photograph.

8. Don't be afraid of silence. You might feel uneasy and want to rush in with another question when your talker stops speaking. *Don't.* Silence is an important part of interviewing, and it can sometimes lead to very interesting results. Because people find silence uncomfortable, they often try to fill it if you don't—and in doing so, they may say something you might not have heard otherwise.

Sometimes silence is also necessary for gathering thoughts. Don't forget—you are asking your subjects to think back on things they may not have considered in years. Calling up these memories may spark other

These two children ended up on a German postcard in 1908.

thoughts, too. Allow your subject time to ponder. You may be thrilled with what he or she remembers.

9. Be ready to ask the same question a few different ways. People don't know how much they know, and rephrasing a question can give you more information. This happens all the time. "I don't know," a relative will tell you, sometimes impatiently. They *do* know—they just don't know that they know. The most common version of this is when an interviewer asks, "What was your father's mother's name?" The relative answers, "I never knew her. I don't know." But a few minutes later, in response to "Whom were you named after?" this answer comes: "My father's mother."

Try to find a couple of ways to ask important questions. You never can be sure what you will learn.

10. Ask to see any family treasures your relatives own. When your talkers bring out an heirloom, ask them to describe what you're looking at. What is it? How was it used? Who made it? Who gave it to them? Ask if there are any stories connected with it, or any documents.

11. Be sensitive to what you discover. Sometimes people become emotional talking about the past. They may remember relatives long dead, or forgotten tragedies. If your talker is upset by a memory, either remain silent, or quietly ask, "Is it all right if we talk some more about this? Or would you rather not?" People frequently feel better when they talk about sad things; you should gently give your relative the *choice* of whether or not to go on.

12. Try not to interrupt. If your talker strays from the subject, let him or her finish the story and then say, "Let's get back to Uncle Moe," or, "You said something earlier about . . ." Not interrupting makes the conversation friendlier, and may lead you to something you didn't expect.

Of course, there is always the exception to the rule. If a story goes on forever and seems useless, the best way to handle it may be to say, "Gee, Aunt Jesse, could you hold the rest of that story for later? I'd like to get the facts out of the way and then come back to that."

13. Ask for songs, poems, unusual memories. You may discover something wonderful when you ask your subject if she recalls the rhymes she used to recite while jumping rope as a little girl, or the hymns she sang in church. Probe a little here—ask about childhood games and memories, smells and tastes and sounds.

When I asked my great-aunt Blima about her childhood in the town of Szrensk, Poland, she told me this:

"I was born the last one. I was the baby. When I was still young, my fa-

A boy's certificate for good behavior in 1880 is a piece of family history today.

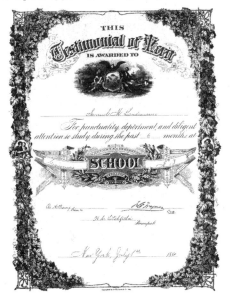

ther went to America and said he would send for my mother and me. We had to make a living while he was gone, so my mother ran a little grocery in the town. She would bake bread, and we sold beer to the people—but it was a little bit undercover, because I don't think we were supposed to sell the beer. I was maybe 13, 14 years old."

"Did you ever drink the beer?" I asked.

"No," she answered, "but I washed my hair with it."

What Questions to Ask

Although you are the expert when it comes to your family and probably know what questions to ask, here are a few suggestions:

● **Home and community life.** "What do you remember about the house you lived in? How many bedrooms did it have? Where did most of the family activities go on? What was the neighborhood (village) like? What kind of people lived there? What did you do for fun? Who else lived in the neighborhood (village, etc.)? What kinds of activities went on there?"

● **Personalities and relationships.** "Tell me about your parents: What kind of people were they? What was most important to them? Did they have a good marriage? What do you remember most vividly about them? What was your relationship like with your mother/father/sister/brother?"

● **Economic conditions.** "How did the family earn money? Who worked? How did your family compare to others in the neighborhood—richer or poorer or in the middle? Who handled the family finances? Were there any major economic setbacks? Were there any big successes? What kinds of things did the family spend money on?"

● **Family characteristics.** "Were there a lot of people in the family who resembled each other? What were the most outstanding family characteristics? Are there any diseases that run in the family? Any physical oddities? Was anyone in our family famous or notorious? Was there a 'black sheep' in the family? Do you remember any big family celebration or event, or a crisis in the family?"

Questions that explore the links between family members can turn up wonderful anecdotes. Be sure to ask about family "characters," and try to get a sense of how they were received within the family.

● **Family facts.** You will always be

Great old family photos may be hidden away in a shoebox.

Back to the Old Country:
Tips on tracing your family across the ocean

Many genealogists call it "crossing the water." That's what you do when you begin to trace your ancestry back to the Old Country.

America is a land of immigrants, and most people have family lines that lead back overseas. The good news is that it *is* possible to research your ancestors' lives in their original nation even without leaving the United States.

Before you attempt to go international, however, get everything you can about your ancestors from American documents (naturalization papers, ships' manifests, etc.) that could be of help to you in tracing your ancestors overseas— they may, for example, list your ancestors' last address in their country of origin or the names and addresses of relatives they left behind.

Techniques and rules are different for each country. If you are seriously interested in researching overseas, you should look for a good genealogical guide to international research (see the list of books in the Appendix).

There are, however, four tips that apply to researching your foreign roots no matter where your ancestors hailed from.

1. Get as much information as you can, from your family and official records, about your ancestors' lives prior to immigration. Absolutely crucial are the names of the village and the province they came from. Add to that any addresses you can discover and any copies of documents.

2. Check with LDS. The best place for any American to start his search for overseas information is with the Church of the Latter-Day Saints (Mormon) Family History Library (see page 144). The LDS collection of genealogical material includes vital records from dozens of nations. There is a good chance that you will find something of interest to you there. In addition, LDS libraries have excellent materials to help you in finding, translating, or deciphering records.

To find an LDS office near you, look in the phone book under "Church of Jesus Christ of Latter-Day Saints," or write to LDS Genealogical Library, 35 North West Temple Street, Salt Lake City, UT 84150.

3. It pays to learn just a bit of your ancestors' original language. In searching foreign records, you do not have to be fluent in another language (though it certainly wouldn't hurt if you were). But if you can pronounce and understand a few words, it may make your work go a lot faster.

4. Join a genealogical society. These groups can be extremely helpful to beginners. For information, check with your local librarian or write (enclose a self-addressed stamped envelope) to the Federation of Genealogical Societies, P.O. Box 220, Davenport, IA 52805. Ask them for the name of the genealogical society near you.

trying to fill in the blanks on your Pedigree Chart and Family Group Sheets. Show your subject the charts and ask: "After whom were you named? Do you know the names of your parents' parents? Do you know anyone who would know more than you do about that branch of the family?

"Where are members of our family buried? Is there a family burial plot? What did great-grandma, etc., die of?"
• **Life in the Old Country and the trip over (for immigrants).** "Tell me why you came to America. Did any member of the family come to America before you? Who, when, and why did they? What did you do when you came here? What kind of work did you do in the Old Country? What kind did you do here? What did you do for entertainment in the Old Country? Did you bring anything special over with you? Why did you choose that item?

"Do you remember anything about your trip to America? Where did you eat, sleep, etc.? Do you remember where you landed? What was your first impression of the United States? Who met you when you arrived?"

If you are lucky enough to have relatives who remember their immigration, question them carefully. There's a lot of richness—and family history—in those memories.

After the Interview

Your interview should not last more than about an hour. People do best when they are not tired. If you think there's more to talk about, schedule another interview. That will give you time to review your notes and consider any other questions you might want to ask. It will also give your relative time to remember more things.

After you've done the interviewing, your hardest, most important work lies ahead. You have to go through the information and analyze it. What have you learned? Did you discover any new relatives, or find out about something worth following up? How accurate is what you have learned?

If you recorded the interview, transcribe it—that is, write or type up the important things your talker told you.

Talk to your older family members; there is no better source for wonderful bits of information about your heritage.

No truth without proof

Aaron Wolfman, the author's father, during World War II.

Although the family stories you hear may be fascinating, they also may not be true. Is there any proof that your ancestor fought in the Civil War, and that he won a medal? If not, then it might be just a wonderful story—not a fact, but a family legend. (Family legends are fine, as long as you label them as such.)

If you don't have proof for a piece of information—where someone was born, what he did in the war—then you can't claim it as a fact.

You may find yourself with two different facts for the same event— like two different birthdates, far apart, for the same person. In that case, you'll have to evaluate the clues and decide which one is right. The important thing is to know where you got each piece of information. Eventually, you'll probably amass enough support material to be able to tell what is valid and what isn't.

A story backed up by a document becomes a "quite-possible" story. Your job is to determine which stories are "possibles," which are "probables," and which sound terrific but are more a testimony to family imagination than family history.

You don't have to note every word Aunt Jesse said—but try to hold on to the *way* she said it. If you didn't record it, but only took notes, rewrite or type them so they're neat and legible.

Review the information. Take out your Family Group Sheets and see if you can add to any of them. Maybe you'll have the name of a third son in a family you'd never heard of, or the address of a home that your grandparents lived in. Write everything in its appropriate place, and be sure to indicate where the information came from. This will come in handy when you want to verify the accuracy of what you've learned.

There's one last, very important step: thanking your talkers. They have been generous with their time, energy, and memories. Sending them a thank-you note and a copy of the interview (for corrections and additions) is a way to show that you value what they've shared.

One of the goals in researching your genealogy is to make your family aware of each other and of their common history. If your relatives' experiences during the interviews are good ones, and if you are thoughtful in showing appreciation, they may be inclined to give you even more help.

CHAPTER SIX

Becoming an American

IMMIGRANTS JUMP INTO THE "MELTING POT"

No one stays an immigrant forever. At some time in your family's history, an ancestor made the transition from newcomer to American.

It was a slow process. It still is.

Imagine how frightening it might feel to live in a new world. You'd be in a place where no one spoke your language, shared your history, or knew your customs. Everything about you would appear strange to other people: the way you dressed, the food you ate, the games you played.

This strangeness made many newcomers feel isolated. That's one reason so many immediately headed for

cities and states where they knew others from their homeland had settled. In those communities, the immigrants could recreate the feeling of the place they had left behind.

Across the United States, hundreds of neighborhoods and cities were miniature versions of the Old Country. Here, immigrants could speak their native language, eat their traditional foods, and live in the familiar, comfortable old style.

Harry Raskolenko was the son of Polish Jewish immigrants. He grew up in one of the world's most crowded immigrant neighborhoods, New York City's Lower East Side. Packed together in that one small community in 1907 were families from Russia, Poland, Italy, and Ireland. Jews, Roman Catholics, and Russian Orthodox lived side by side. And yet . . .

"All of us had our special places, dictated to us by our faces, our speech, our jobs, our music, dances, and books—and of course, our religion and country of origin," Raskolenko recalled. "Each one lived in a ghetto within a ghetto. . . . We wanted to be among our own people, our own language, our own religion, and to be ourselves down to our last Jewish roots."

The street was a busy marketplace in poor immigrant neighborhoods. Above, New York City's Lower East Side around 1900.

Where they settled

In looking for your ancestors, it may be helpful to keep in mind where different national groups went. Here is a listing of some of the many groups who came to America, and some of the places where they tended to live:

African-Americans: Southeast; later, big cities of mid-Atlantic and midwestern states

Arab-Americans: New York; Los Angeles; Detroit

Armenians: New York; Massachusetts; Rhode Island; California

Basques: Nevada; southeast Oregon; southwest Idaho

Belgians: Detroit; eastern Wisconsin

Chinese: San Francisco; Los Angeles; New York City; Honolulu

Cubans: Miami and south Florida; New York City area

Czechs and Slovaks: Prairie populations in Wisconsin, Nebraska, and Texas; urban populations in New York, Chicago, Cleveland, St. Louis, Pittsburgh

Dominicans: New York City; also Chicago, Massachusetts, Florida

Dutch: Hudson Valley, New York, and New Jersey coast; later, many moved to California and Michigan, especially Grand Rapids and Holland

English: Atlantic seaboard, north and south

Filipinos: San Francisco; Los Angeles; Seattle

Finnish: Midwest, especially Michigan and Minnesota; California; New York

French Canadians: Mill and factory towns of New England

French Huguenots: South Carolina; New Rochelle, New York; Rhode Island

Germans: Northeast; Midwest, especially Wisconsin, Illinois, Indiana, Iowa

Greeks: Northeastern and midwestern cities, particularly New York and Chicago

Haitians: New York City

Hungarians: Pennsylvania; industrial midwestern cities like Chicago, Akron, Toledo, Milwaukee, Detroit

Indians (from India): New York; California

Irish: Northeastern big cities, especially New York and Boston

Italians: Northeastern and mid-Atlantic cities, especially New York and Philadelphia; California

Japanese: Hawaii; California; Washington; Oregon

Koreans: California; New York; Hawaii; Washington

Mexicans: California; Texas; Arizona; New Mexico

Norwegians: Midwest, especially rural areas

Poles: Midwestern cities, especially Chicago, Cleveland, Pittsburgh, Buffalo

Portuguese: New England states, especially Massachusetts; New Jersey

Russians: New York; Pennsylvania; Illinois; New England

Russian (eastern European) Jews: East Coast cities, with a concentration in the New York City area

Swedes: New York State; Minnesota; Illinois; Washington; California

Swiss: California's famous Swiss colony; northern and central Ohio

Welsh: Mining towns in Pennsylvania and Ohio

The drive to share "immigrant roots" created many new communities. "Little Italys" and "Irishtowns" sprung up in cities across the Northeast. Thousands of Dutch newcomers settled in southwestern Michigan cities. A Norwegian immigrant who wanted to farm in the Great Plains would head toward Iowa or Minnesota because both those states had large Norwegian populations.

Living with countrymen and women made it easier to socialize and to feel a part of a community. In those neighborhoods, it was simpler to meet a prospective husband or wife, to shop for familiar foods. You could be sure there would be a place to buy newspapers written in your language, and that you'd find a church or synagogue just like the one you'd left on the other side of the ocean.

For immigrants who felt nervous in their new country, these neighborhoods also offered protection. The Chinese who immigrated to America during the 1850s and '60s encountered a great deal of prejudice from white Americans. Living together in "Chinatowns" not only made for an easier life, but it also gave the inhabitants a greater sense of security.

Because these neighborhoods were so filled with the flavor of the Old Country, it was possible to spend your whole life in America and never really become Americanized. There are many stories of immigrants from Italy or Puerto Rico or Russia who came to the United States when they were young, lived here for 40, 50, or 60 years, and yet, after all that time, could speak almost no English! They didn't need to—everything could be done in the neighborhood using the old language.

That way of life appealed to some immigrants, those who felt lonely and homesick for the old way of life. To many, however, the Old World was the past. By coming to America, they had entered the future. Now it was time to become something new and different: an "American."

In 1908, the playwright Israel

In 1892, immigrant shopkeepers posed in front of their store in San Francisco's Chinatown.

Immigrant children pledge allegiance to the flag in 1889. Kids often became "American-ized" more quickly than their parents.

Zangwill called America "the great Melting Pot, where all the races of Europe are melting and reforming." Zangwill believed that America was the place where all the peoples of the Old World would lose their hatreds and their rivalries. He hoped that coming to America would change things, that prejudice and old feuds would disappear. "These are the fires of God," he wrote in his play, also called *The Melting Pot*. "Germans and Frenchmen, Irishmen and Englishmen, Jews and Russians—into the Crucible with you all! God is making the American."

The idea of the melting pot was irresistible to many people. Immigrants saw it promising acceptance: I am an American, someone who belongs here, not just a visitor from a country across the sea. To long-time Americans, it promised an end to the confusing and strange differences the immigrants brought with them.

The melting pot notion sounded good, but it had one important flaw. Many immigrants didn't want to see all of their past simply melt away. Although they had left their homelands, they were still proud of their cultures, their customs, and their religions—and were not about to throw away long-held traditions. Instead, they combined them with American customs and created their own mixture. They became Americans, but Americans who had a past as well as a future.

Making the Adjustment

Few people could afford, or wanted, to spend all their time in their neighborhood. Adults went to work. Kids went to school. They made new friends, learned new ways, and learned to speak and read English. Over time, they began to understand how America worked. But it wasn't easy.

Many children had not been able to go to school in the Old Country because they had to work with their parents. In America, children *had* to go to school—it was required by law.

"I went to public school and . . . I had a miserable time. I would come home and cry and say, 'I don't understand them and they don't understand me,' " remembered Josephine Reale, who spoke only Italian when she arrived in Philadelphia at age five. "I learned very fast, though. Before I knew it I could speak as well as the other kids," she added, with a laugh. "And we got along fine. . . . I began to like this country."

The new immigrants expected life in

An immigrant boy takes a bath and washes his underwear at the same time.

this country to be very different from life in their homeland, but nothing could have prepared them for many of the changes.

Most families came from small villages and farms in Europe. Now they were learning what it was like to live in cramped apartment buildings in noisy, crowded, and dirty cities.

In the Old Country, most people worked long hours just to feed their families. Many worked in the fields. In this new world, the people worked long hours in factories, mines, or mills, doing exhausting, dangerous work.

In the big American cities like New York, Philadelphia, Boston, and Chicago, male and female immigrants working in the clothing industry were packed into small, crowded rooms for 10 or 12 hours every day. The conditions in these rooms were so terrible that a new word, "sweatshop," was invented to describe them.

As they worked, immigrants learned more "American" ways. Their clothing began to change. The colorful costumes of European farmers and peasants soon disappeared, replaced by the more functional coat and jacket of the workingman. Beards began to disappear, too. American men were mostly clean-shaven, and quickly, so were many European-born men. For women, mass-produced dresses and stylish hats replaced the handmade outfits and shawls that European women used to wear.

Children brought many changes into their homes. Often parents learned English more slowly than their kids, who picked up "Americanisms" right away in school. Kids were also quick to copy American dress styles and to pick up American games. Soon the sons of Italian fishermen and Russian farmers were practicing baseball and basketball on city streets, and their daughters were playing jacks and jump rope.

Food was another great Americanizer. When immigrants sat down to eat, they discovered the *real* melting pot. At first, of course, all families ate

The cramped tenement life of an immigrant family in Chicago, around 1910.

A countryman's helping hand: Immigrant aid societies

Where could new immigrants go when they needed financial assistance during their early days in America? Banks were often nervous about lending money to these poor new arrivals. And besides, banks charged a lot of interest.

Family members, of course, helped each other, and so did friends. But sometimes a new American needed more assistance than family or friends could give. In these cases, many newcomers turned to a group of countrymen: self-help groups known as "immigrant aid societies."

These aid societies were run *by* immigrants *for* immigrants. Most offered financial assistance and job-hunting advice. Others collected and forwarded mail for their members, arranged social events like dances and parties, or helped immigrants find apartments. Some even ran summer camps for their members' children!

Many societies were large organizations for anyone who came from the Old Country. They carried names like the Danish Brotherhood in America or the Ukrainian Alliance of America. One group, the Russian Orthodox Catholic Mutual Aid Society, had 138 branches in 17 states and Canada. Other groups were smaller, made up of people who emigrated from the same city, town, or village. The Chmielniker Sick and Benevolent Society, for example, was a *landsmanshaft* organized in 1905 by Jewish immigrants from the tiny Polish village of Chmielnik to offer aid to any "landsmen" (persons from the same community) who needed it (*shaft* means "organization"). Chinese *hui* and Japanese *kenjinkan* were self-help groups usually organized by immigrants from the same home province.

These groups recruited members on the streets of immigrant neighborhoods or in the churches or synagogues of the community. Each member paid dues to the group. Although each individual amount was small, it turned into a mighty sum when multiplied by the number of members. The total was a kind of community insurance policy, enough to help members in need.

When Hans needed money to start a business, he might ask the Sons of Norway for a loan. If Giuseppe's wife died unexpectedly, he might be given a grant by the Calabrian Emigrants Organization to pay for the funeral. Heinrich might buy life insurance through the Order of the Sons of Herman in the State of Texas; Kryztyna might find a job with the help of the Association of Polish Women of the United States; and if Blima were looking for a nice boy to go out with, she might attend the dances organized by the Jewish *Arbeiter Ring* (Workmen's Circle).

There were thousands of these groups in the early 20th century, when so many immigrants arrived in America. But they are not a thing of the past. Today, many new groups have been formed as the latest wave of immigrants have created their own self-help organizations. The nationalities may now be Hispanic and Vietnamese and East Indian, but the help they're offering would be familiar to any former member of a *kenjinkan* or a *landsmanshaft*.

only what they had eaten in the Old Country. They were suspicious of other types of food.

But slowly, they began to experiment. Mary Antin, who arrived in America from Russia in 1893, wrote about her very first American meal: "My father produced several kinds of food, ready to eat, without any cooking, from little tin cans that had printing all over them. He attempted to introduce us to a queer, slippery kind of fruit, which he called 'banana.'" The family refused to eat this strange new fruit, however, and Mary's dad finally gave up his experiment.

Over time, "foreign" foods turned familiar. Italians sampled something called a bagel. Kids whose parents were born in Bristol or Oslo or Dublin or Kiev gobbled up a flat baked bread with cheese and tomato on it. Soon, there were pizza parlors on city street corners. The children of Chinese immigrants learned to like German delicacies called frankfurters.

The power of the immigrant neighborhood lasted for many years. But ever so slowly, things changed. The children of immigrants went on to get better educations than their parents had. They became businesspeople, doctors, lawyers, teachers, and moved

New York City's Lower East Side neighborhood has been home to many waves of immigrants. In this 1970s photo, neighborhood kids are about to beat the summer heat with some cool ices.

out of the old neighborhood. In many cases, their parents moved with them. In other cases, the parents kept the old neighborhood alive.

Things have constantly been changing in Harry Raskolenko's Lower East Side. In the 1850s, it was filled with German and Irish newcomers. When they moved out by the 1880s, Italian and eastern European Jewish families moved in, along with Romanians, Hungarians, Greeks, Poles, Turks, and Slovaks. In the 1940s, the Jews and Italians began leaving and large numbers of Hispanic immigrants started making the area their home.

The cycle repeats itself over and over. A poor immigrant group comes into the neighborhood, works and saves its money, and eventually moves to a more prestigious area. As that group leaves, another group moves in.

Over the past decade, the last of the eastern European Jewish community has begun disappearing from the Lower East Side. The newest groups—thousands and thousands of Chinese, Vietnamese, and Koreans—have been moving in.

The Lower East Side today is filled with different languages, foods, and houses of worship than it was 150, 100, or even 50 years ago. Many of the residents are immigrants or the children of immigrants, but the neighborhood in many ways has remained the same—bustling, noisy, and crowded with the sights and smells of far-off lands. It is a model "entry community," a spectacular mirror of 150 years of immigrant history.

There are Lower East Side-type communities in big cities all over the United States. Each is a kind of launching pad, a place where people on the way up live while they work to better themselves and their families. As long as they serve as doors for people moving on up, these neighborhoods will continue to be a vital part of the American immigrant experience.

CHAPTER SEVEN

The Name Game

THE HISTORY AND MEANING OF FAMILY NAMES

"**H**ello," the man in the white coat said as he walked into the room. "I'm Bill Doctor." It took a minute to sink in. Was this man really called "Dr. Doctor"?

Yes, he admitted with a good-natured shrug. "If someone asks, 'Is there a doctor in the house?' I guess I should answer twice."

Why is that funny? What makes us laugh if we meet a Judy Tailor who works as a tailor, or a Billy Baker who specializes in cakes? What makes us

do a double-take when we see a sign that reads "Law Offices of Ellen M. Law"?

There is one simple reason: We don't expect names to *mean* anything. But they do. Names are filled with meaning, symbolism, and history. First and middle names frequently have family tradition behind them. Family names may reveal where ancestors lived, what they looked like, how they acted or spoke, how they earned a living, or who their parents were.

Start with your own name. Do you know the original family names of your four grandparents? They probably hint at the country (or countries) your family comes from, but their meanings may be hidden from you because the names are in the language of your relatives' original homeland.

Even if you don't know the meaning of your ancestors' names, there are ways to go about deciphering them. In the Appendix, you'll find a dictionary of almost 400 last names adapted from the *New Dictionary of American Family Names*. You may find one or more of your own family names there. "What's in a Name?" on page 107 offers more suggestions on how to proceed in your name search.

What kind of work did your ancestors do? Your last name may be a clue.

Tracing the History of Names

Last names are a modern invention. From the earliest days of human beings until recently, people across the world only had one name. They were John or Ivan, Abdul or Shoshana, Sese or Haile, Isabella or Roberto—and that was enough. Parents gave children unique names, made up just for them. Almost everyone lived in the countryside or in villages with very small populations, so one name suited most folks just fine.

But as the years went on, villages grew larger and became towns. Towns turned into cities. Some people began naming their children after famous heroes or religious figures.

As a result, many towns had people with the same name. In 14th-century England, for example, it is estimated that two out of every three men in the country had one of five names—Henry, William, Robert, John, and Richard. This made for some pretty interesting situations.

Imagine an English village around that time. Someone new arrives in town and asks a native, "Excuse me, but where can I find William?"

"Which William?" the native responds.

The visitor looks blank. "*Which* William?"

The native decides to help: "Are you looking for William who has a house at the lake? Or William whose father is that loud rascal Jack? Or maybe you mean William who runs the mill? Or the William who has the flaming red hair?"

Suddenly, a light goes on in the visitor's eyes. "I want William the farmer, the father of two young girls named Rebecca and Roxanne. I believe he has red hair, yes."

"Why didn't you say so?" the by-now impatient townsman says, and then directs the newcomer to William the Red-Haired's home. (William couldn't have just given out his ad-

First names

Where did your first name come from? Were you named after someone special? Is your name part of a family naming tradition?

You may not be aware of it, but your first name is loaded with meaning. Your parents thought long and hard before choosing it.

In the earliest days of naming, parents often chose names that would bless their children with special qualities. Faith, Hope, and Grace are just three examples among English-language names. (Ann is a Hebrew name that means "grace.") In American colonial times, daughters in particular ended up with names like Patience and Charity.

Boys' names also carried meanings, but many of them have been lost to us. Robert means "famous" or "bright"; Peter means "rock"; Curtis, "courteous"; Seth, "the appointed one"; Richard, "powerful ruler"; and Donald, "world ruler."

First names also have meanings *within* families. Certain names occur again and again in one family's history. For example, in some families first-born sons are named after the father or grandfather. In Catholic families, names may be taken from saints. And Jewish parents frequently name their children after relatives who have recently died.

These naming patterns may be genealogical clues. Be sure to ask all your family members what they know about their own first names.

What's in a name?

There are over 1.6 million names in the United States, and each one has its own history. Here's how to begin to search for yours.

• **Is it original?** Before you do anything else, find out if the names you are researching—your last name, for example, or those of your grandparents—are the ones your ancestors brought with them to this country. Many have been altered. Immigrants themselves probably made many changes in order to feel more American or to try to avoid prejudice. Sometimes, immigration clerks made mistakes with difficult (for them) foreign spellings, like Andrjuljawierjus, Grzyszczyszn, Koutsoghianopolous, and Zemiszkicicicz.

Whatever the reason, you want to know about the change and, if you can, find out not only how but also why it occurred. This may give you a good story, or a personal insight into your ancestors.

Start by asking your parents or your oldest relatives. They may even know the precise spelling of Old Country versions of your family names.

• **What language is it in?** You proba-

Immigrants' names often changed soon after arrival.

bly know the ethnic heritage and language of your last name. If for any reason you don't, your parents should be able to tell you.

Once you know which language your name comes from, you can look it up in a dictionary of that language. The translation may tell you right off what your name means—or at least hint at the meaning.

• **Check the list in the Appendix.** There are nearly 400 names in this list, and you may be lucky enough to find yours there. But if you need to keep looking, consult the classic book on the subject, Elsdon C. Smith's *New Dictionary of American Family Names*. It includes nearly 20,000 names!

• **Still can't locate your name?** Try saying it out loud in different ways. This requires some imagination. Many names are approximations of the originals, because strange things happened to immigrants' names as they made their way to America. Often, the names changed because English-speaking clerks had problems with the sounds of foreign languages.

For example, Janos is pronounced Yan-osh in Czech; it could easily have ended up being spelled that way. W's in German are pronounced "V"; Weber could have easily turned into Vayber.

So be on the lookout for these letters, which may have been confused or changed: F/V; W/V; B/V; P/B; J/Y.

dress because in medieval England, streets did not have names and numbers. And besides, most people couldn't read).

Scenes like this became increasingly common. More and more natives ended up describing their neighbors. Soon, within the town, people didn't just say "William" anymore—they automatically referred to "William whose house is at the Lake," "William son of Jack," "William the Miller," and "William the Red."

Over time, long-winded phrases such as "whose house is at the" were dropped, and only "William Lake" remained. William, Jack's son, became William Jackson; William the Miller became William Miller; and William the Red became William Russell, the Old English word for "red-haired." Last names had arrived.

The growth of family names spread over the next few hundred years. Governments began insisting that people take second names because they needed those names to tax their citizens and draft young men into their armies.

But as late as 1800, many people were still without surnames. It was only over the course of the next 100 years that countries in eastern Europe and Scandinavia finally insisted that their people adopt permanent family names.

Four Kinds of Names

Permanent names were decided upon in a few ways. In many cases, people chose the ones they wanted, then the government recorded it. Other times, officials picked the names for them.

Names often came about naturally. A man or woman was given a nickname in addition to his first name, the nickname stuck, and it was eventually adopted as a permanent name that was passed on from father to son. Daughters were expected to take dad's surname until they married; then they were to take their husband's name. And that's the way it has been until recently (see "Something New in Naming" on page 112).

But where did all those last names come from? Let's go back to the medieval English village and its many Williams. Their names came from one of four sources:

● **Patronymics.** The father's name with "son" immediately after it.
● **Place names.** Words that identified where a person lived.
● **Occupational names.** What a

Mr. Smith got his name from working with metal.

person did for a living.
● **Nicknames.** Names based on a person's characteristics (personality or appearance).

There is an excellent chance your name comes from one of these four types, because they account for more than 90 percent of the names in America today. Here are some examples.

Patronymics are carried by about one in every four Americans. There

The mighty Smith

The most common family name in the world is Chang. More than 75 million Chinese carry that moniker. But the name that is most common in Western countries is—are you surprised?—Smith.

There are somewhere in the vicinity of 3.3 million Smiths in the United States; at least 500,000 in England and Wales; nearly 100,000 in Scotland; more than 75,000 in Canada; over 30,000 in Ireland; and probably another 50,000 in Australia and New Zealand. In each of those countries, about 1 out of every 100 people is named Smith.

The name Smith comes from the Old English word *smite*, which means "to strike." Smiths worked with metals, using hammers or other tools to smite the metal and make something useful like horseshoes, plows, tools, or swords. These implements were important to the people in the village, which must have made Smith a prominent figure in town.

That must be part of the reason why in every nation there are people whose names translate as "Smith." For example:

Arabic: *Haddad*
Armenian: *Darbinian*
Bulgarian: *Kovac*
Catalan: *Feffer*
Czech: *Kovar*
Dutch: *Smid, Smidt, Smit, Smed*
Estonian: *Raudsepp, Kalevi*
Finnish: *Rautio, Seppanen*
French: *Lefevre, Lefebvre, Ferrier, Ferron, Faure*
German: *Schmidt, Schmitt, Schmid, Schmitz*
Greek: *Skmiton*
Gypsy: *Petulengro*
Hungarian: *Kovacs*

Irish Gaelic: *Gough, Goff*
Italian: *Feffaro, Ferraro*
Norwegian: *Smid*
Persian: *Ahangar*
Polish: *Kowal*
Portuguese: *Ferreiro*
Romanian: *Covaciu*
Russian: *Kuznetsov, Koval*
Spanish: *Herrera*
Swedish: *Smed*
Turkish: *Temirzi*
Welsh: *Goff, Gowan*

There are also a number of specialized Smiths: Mr. Goldsmith, Mr. Hammersmith, and Mr. Naismith (he made nails). And in addition to the millions of just plain Smiths in the United States, there are Smithers, Smithsons, and Smythes. All of them were workers in metal, or children of those workers.

Amidst all those metal-minded people, there is one Smith type whose ancestors may have never picked up a hammer. Smithfields got their names from a location. In Old English, the name means "smooth field."

Daddy's boys:
Patronymics around the world

Here is a list of the attachments (mostly endings) that indicate "son of" or "ancestor of" in other languages, plus examples of how they are used:

acs, Hungarian; descendant of (Lukacs, descendant of Luke)

aitis, onis, Lithuanian; son of (Gerulaitis, son of Gero)

ak, ack, Polish; descendant of (Agustyniak, descendant of August)

akis, akos, Greek; descendant of (Theodorakis, descendant of Theodore)

Ap, Welsh; son of, comes before the name (Ap Richard turned into Pritchard, Ap Owen into Bowen, Ap Howell into Powell)

Ben, Hebrew; son of, comes before the name (Ben Gurion, Ben Yehuda)

chuk, chik, Ukrainian; descendant of (Kovalchik, Adamchuk)

enku, Ukrainian; son of (Shevchenko, son of Shevcho)

es, Portuguese; son of (Lopes, son of Lope)

escu, Romanian; of our family (Romanescu, Antonescu)

ez, Spanish; son of (Perez, son of Pedro, Juarez, son of Juan)

Fitz, English (Norman); son of, comes before the name (FitzGerald)

ian, Armenian; son of (Khatchaturian, Manoogian)

Ibn, Arabic; son of, comes before the name (Yusuf Ibn Khalid, son of Khalid)

O', Irish (Gaelic); descendant, or grandson, of (O'Connor, O'Keith)

ov, Slavic (Russian, etc); son of (Romonoff, Romanov)

Mac, Scottish; descendant of (MacDougal)

Mc, Irish; descendant of (McGlynn)

poulous, Greek; son of (Andropolous, son of Andros)

s, English; son of (Edwards, Williams, Peters, Adams)

sen, Norwegian; also Danish; son of (Peterssen, Carlssen)

sohn, German; son of (Mendelsohn, Sarasohn)

son, Swedish; son of (Swenson)

vich, Russian; son of (Denisovich)

vici, Romanian, Serbian; son of (Marcovici)

wiecz, wicz, Polish; son of (Karkowicz)

zoon, Dutch; son of (Anderzoon)

are numerous English names like this: Bill, son of Robert, became Bill Robertson or Robinson. Likewise Wilson, Johnson, Jameson, Jackson. There are a few cases in which names were given after the mother—Allison (Alice's son) is one English-language example—but they are rare.

Sometimes a father's name was adopted with just an "s" at the end: Peters, James, Rogers. There are even some cases where the father's name was adopted as is: Robert, son of George, became Robert George; Tommy, son of John, became Tommy John.

The word patronymic comes from the Latin word *pater*, which means "father." Patronymics occur in most European languages. In Sweden, Norway, Denmark, and German-speaking countries, it's easy to spot: Hansen is Hans' son; and Ludwig's son is Ludwigsohn. In Spanish, the ending *ez* indicates "son of"—as in Rodriguez and Fernandez, the sons of Rodrigo and Fernando.

In Slavic countries (Russia, Poland, Lithuania, Yugoslavia, Czechoslovakia), "son of" is indicated by a variation of *ov*, *vich*, or *wicz*: Romanov, Ivanovich, and Janowicz are the sons of Roman, Ivan, and Janos.

John Porter of H⁄ = JOHN PORTER (son) OF HENRY
John Ellor (Jacob Son) = JOHN ELLOR (JACOB SON)
John Wood (of John) = JOHN WOOD (son) (of John)
John Wood of James = JOHN WOOD (son) of James
John McLeod Self + Estate = JOHN McLEOD SELF AND ESTATE
Jonathan + Wm Eady = JONATHAN AND WILLIAM EADY

On this old list, you see permanent family names and patronymics, like Jacobson on line two.

For a list of different ways that indicate "son of" or, occasionally, "ancestor of" in other languages, see "Daddy's Boys" on the opposite page.

Place names. More than 40 percent of all Americans have names that have to do with a location. There are two types of these names: One had to do with a physical description of the local resident's home; the other was adopted for people who moved in from another town or country.

A "local" name came from the physical characteristics of the land where someone lived. For example, William who lived at the Hill became William Hill. If he lived at the Marsh, William Marsh. And if William lived near a great gathering of trees, he might have been dubbed Forest or Woods.

The same thing held true in many other languages. In German, Mr. Woods would have been Mr. Wald; in French, Mr. DuBois; in Italian, Mr. Bosco.

A "long-distance" name had to do with the town or country from which someone came. If Heinrich moved from Vienna to another city, his neighbors might refer to him as Heinrich from Vienna (Wien)—or, in German, Heinrich Wiener. This is how many names came about: the Italian Di Napoli (from Naples), the Russian Minsky (from Minsk), the German Sulzberger (from Salzberg), and the English Sunderland (from the southern lands of Scotland), for example.

Occupational names are carried by about 15 percent of Americans. People commonly took these names from their work: butchers, bakers, butlers, tailors, etc. James the Baker became James Baker; James the Tailor became James Taylor.

Mr. Tailor would be Signore Sartori in Italian, Herr Schneider in German, Monsieur Tailleur in French, and Pan Krawczyk in Polish. Baker is Becker in German, Piekarz in Polish, Fornari in Italian, and Boulanger in French.

Occasionally, women get their due in this area. A few occupational surnames are specifically female, and were probably given to a family where the woman was well known for her talent. Baxter was a female baker; Thaxter was a woman known for her work thatching roofs.

Nicknames. This fourth type of surname, based on personal characteristics, is held by about 15 percent of all Americans. To this day, people get nicknames for their personality traits

Something new in naming

For the last few hundred years, there was a strict rule about surnames: Men had the enduring ones, and women followed.

A single woman carried her father's name and when she married, she took her husband's last name. Bill James's daughter Sue was known as Sue James. When she married Bob Jones, she instantly turned into Sue Jones.

There were a few occasions when famous female last names would be preserved. If Jack Nobody married Linda Distinguished—who came from a wealthy and well-respected family—sometimes Jack would take on Linda's last name. In Great Britain, the solution to this problem was to attach the woman's high-class name to the man's: Armstrong-Jones, Coverly-Smith, Scott-Moncrieff.

But in most of Western society, the male name was the one that survived. Until the 1960s, that is. As more women went on to careers of their own, they began to resist losing their names. Should a well-known painter, lawyer, doctor, or engineer change her name overnight because she married? If a woman had worked hard to build up a good name in her field, why give it up?

Two solutions were arrived at. One was that old British standard, the hyphenated name, a joining of both families. If Ann Slocum married Peter Sayers, she could become Ann Slocum-Sayers. The children could then be named either Sayers or Slocum-Sayers.

The other solution was simpler. "I'll keep my name; you keep yours." So Ann Slocum remained Ann Slocum, and she would say, "I'd like you to meet my husband, Peter Sayers." Generally, the kids would still take the father's last name.

In the 1990s, the second solution seems to be the more popular one. Many women still take their husband's names, and some women and men create hyphenated offspring. But the easiest solution has turned out, for many, to be the best.

(Wild Willie) or their physical attributes (Big Mike). You may have had—or given—one of those names yourself. When surnames were being taken, some people ended up with nicknames that have lasted hundreds of years. Here are some examples from Old English names: Hardy, Short, and Long refer to physical characteristics; Goodman, Savage, and Truman refer to the individual's personality.

Other European languages follow the same pattern. Hungarian Mr. Nagy (big) was a large fellow; Germans must have thought Lustig was a happy guy; the Poles regarded Mr. Halas as a noisy, bustling type; and the French thought Mr. Belcher was . . . no, not rude, but *bel cher*, or "well-loved."

Hundreds of negative names were given out, but many of them have disappeared because people chose to change their names to something more pleasing. In other cases, the negative meaning has been lost over the years.

Those negative meanings often have nothing to do with the characteristics of people today. Think about this: Kennedy means "large or ugly head" in Irish Gaelic, and Bouvier, Jacqueline Kennedy Onassis's family name, means "cow herder" in French.

So names reveal the past, but don't determine the present. They are history, not destiny.

Other Types of Names

In addition to these four major types, there are a number of other kinds of names in the United States today.

Asian names generally don't follow the standard Western patterns. In China, where surnames have a very long history, they are almost always one-syllable words that may be taken after the name of an old ruling family (Song) or a verb like Tung (to correct). There are few occupational or location names. Vietnamese names like Ky, Thieiu, and Nguyen grow out of the Chinese tradition.

In Japan, names were created more recently out of two unrelated, often poetic words. Suzuki means "bell" and "tree," Nakada means "middle" and "rice field"; Nakamura means "middle" and "village."

Jewish names sometimes are made up of acronyms, abbreviations that combine a number of words. The common Katz often comes from *kohen tzedek*, two Hebrew words that mean "righteous priest." Segal, also Cha-gall, stands for *segan leviah*, meaning "priest of righteousness." And Schatz comes from *shaliah tzibur*, Hebrew for "representative of the congregation."

African names have been very rare in America until recently. Most slaves were forced to take names that their masters were comfortable with. As a result, many African-American surnames today are of British origin, reflecting their masters' backgrounds.

But of late, there has been a return by some African-Americans to ancestral names. LeRoi Jones and Paulette Williams both changed their names; they are now the well-known writers Amiri Baraka and Ntozake Shange.

Other African-Americans have taken names that reflect their conversion to the religion of Islam. Boxer Cassius Clay is now world famous as Muhammad Ali, and basketball star Lew Alcindor changed his name to Kareem Abdul-Jabbar.

The names all around you are filled with meaning. Write down your friends' names. Can you figure out their origins, their meanings? The United States is a great country for studying names—thanks to immigrants from so many nations.

CHAPTER EIGHT

The Paper Chase

HOW TO FIND—AND USE—DOCUMENTS ABOUT YOUR FAMILY

Whenever I played at my grandparents' house as a child, two very serious people watched me in silence. No matter what I did, they never spoke, but they were always there, observing me.

They were portraits—large, hand-colored portraits—of a man and a woman, and they hung on the walls of my father's parents' living room.

The man had a stern, solemn look. His beard was long and straight and white, and he wore a dark jacket and black hat. The woman was serious-looking, too. She had high cheekbones, deep dark eyes, and wore a

We'd always known great-grandpa's full name, but . . .

. . . great-grandma's was a mystery until we found a document.

either. In fact, no one remembered anything about her.

That seemed to be the end of it. No one knew her name, and I guessed I never would, either. But one day I did find it out—with the help of the city of New York. In an office in lower Manhattan was a copy of a wedding license that my grandfather and grandmother had filled out in 1909. And there, on the license, were the names of the parents of the bride and groom—including that of my great-grandmother, Slava Shapiro.

It felt good to read those two words. Now the proud face on the wall once again had a name.

This is one small example of the importance of learning how to use public documents.

Facts about *your* family are just sitting on shelves and in file cabinets and desk drawers, waiting for you to find them. As a genealogist, one of your jobs will be figuring out how to get at those facts.

There are hundreds of places where information about your family may be found, because from the moment your ancestors set foot in America, someone was writing down their names. Did they arrive on a ship, by bus, or by plane? There's probably a record of it

black shawl around her head. Something about her was tough, strong, and proud. I wasn't surprised to learn they were my great-grandparents—my grandfather's mother and father.

When I became interested in genealogy, I started to ask more about these stern faces who now hung on the wall of my parents' den. What were their names? Had they ever come to America?

No, my father told me, they never came to America; they lived and died in Russia. The man's name was the same as my father's; dad had been named after his grandfather. But my father didn't know his grandmother's full name, and no one else seemed to,

somewhere. Did they get married, divorced, have children, die? Forms had to be filled out, and those forms are on file in some office. Did they apply for American citizenship, a passport, social security? Did they ever vote? Somewhere in the United States, there are records of all of that. And the information on these records can help you find out a great deal about the people in your past.

The most important documents for genealogists are:
- Vital records (birth, marriage, and death certificates)
- Religious records
- Cemetery records
- Census forms

This piece of paper made an immigrant feel very proud: his certificate of naturalization.

- Citizenship papers
- Passenger ship lists
- Military records
- Other records like school records, deeds, and wills

You'll want to track down these records because they often have information that no one remembers. A copy of your grandmother's birth certificate, for example, might tell you about her parents—your great-grandparents—that grandma herself has forgotten. A copy of a long-gone ancestor's marriage license may hold clues to relatives even further back.

You will find these documents by writing to, or visiting, records centers, libraries, archives, government offices, and courthouses. In some cases, you will be able to look at the documents yourself; in other cases, you will have to pay a small fee and let other people look for you.

This process is called a "document search." You'll be surprised at how many different kinds of documents there are, and how many places you may have to search to find the ones you're looking for. Some of the records may be photocopied or on microfilm. Other places may have the original paper, signed by your ancestor, and it may be 100 or more years old.

Ten Tips Before You Begin Your Search

Before you start looking for your ancestors' documents, there are 10 points you should keep in mind:

1. In order to find most personal records, you need to know *where* someone lived and *when* certain events happened. Documents are generally kept near where an event happened. For example, birth certificates are usually on file in cities where the birth took place. Immigration papers are often kept in the cities where the immigrant landed. If you don't know where and (approximately) when something happened, you will have difficulty finding most records.

2. If your ancestor had a common

name, you'll need extra information. If you know that your grandfather was named John Smith and that he was born in Brooklyn, New York, in 1923, you really don't know enough. You'll have to have an address, an exact date, and/or both of his parents' names, including his mother's maiden name (let's hope that they weren't John and Mary Smith).

3. You can use one document to lead you to another. Sometimes information on one document refers to another document. For example, your grandfather's citizenship papers may tell you which boat he arrived on, and when—which could help you in your search for a copy of the ship's manifest. Or your grandmother's birth certificate may tell you the date of your great-grandparents' marriage—which can lead you to their marriage license.

4. Always enclose a self-addressed, stamped envelope (SASE) when you write for genealogical help. This has become an expected courtesy among genealogists. By including an envelope with a stamp and your address already on it, you make it easier for the recipient to just drop a reply in the mail. That means you'll probably get a faster response.

Old postcards make your ancestors' hometowns come alive. This is a view of Albany, New York, in the early 1900s.

5. When asking for a document in person or by mail, give just the relevant facts. Don't talk about your entire family history. Just explain exactly what you are looking for, giving enough information to make it clear. Here's an example of a letter you might send to a city bureau of records:

"I'd like a copy of the birth certificate for John Jones, who was born in Kansas City in the month of June, 1876. His parents were Elvira and Jojo Jones. I have enclosed a self-addressed, stamped envelope."

6. Keep a calendar listing your research. It's a good idea to keep a "research log." This will help you keep track of what you've already done and what still needs to be done.

7. If a records center is near you, try to visit it—but *always* call before you go. Make sure that the records you want are there, that the office is open when you want to go, and that they will let you in. Ask if you will have to pay for photocopies. Nothing is more frustrating than going to the wrong place—or to the right place at the wrong time (see "Checklist: Before You Go to a Records Center" on page 133).

8. Handle everything carefully. If you are allowed to examine original records, you may come across fragile old books that could chip, flake, or even fall apart. These records are precious to many people besides you, so handle them as gently as you can. Try to leave them in the same condition as you found them.

9. If you can't make a photocopy of the record, extract the important information. Some records cannot be photocopied. They may be too old, or a photocopier may not be available.

Don't think you have to write down every word. Many documents are very long and filled with legal jargon and unimportant phrases. The best thing to do in these cases is to read the document slowly and thoroughly. Then carefully write down all identifying numbers and important information.

If you end up looking at the same kind of document—like citizenship papers or land deeds—very often, you

Helen Rabkin's birth certificate tells how old her parents were, what work they did, and where they lived.

may want to make up an "abstract" of that kind of document. An abstract is like a shopping list—it will help you remember what you're looking for when you do a document search. Write down the information you expect to see, leaving blank spaces for filling in the specific information you discover on each document. You'll find an abstract for citizenship papers in the Appendix.

10. Look over every document with a skeptical eye. It's exciting to find an ancestor's old records. You may discover some new and interesting information. But as in all your Ancestor Detector work, don't assume that because a piece of data is in print, it's accurate. You've got to evaluate what's in front of you. Who filled out the form? (It's usually more trustworthy if the person himself wrote the information down.) Does it match other information you have? Are there "facts" that contradict what you already know? Which "fact" is then more accurate?

You play judge and jury here. Weigh the evidence and decide what you can trust. Then take the information from the document and transfer it to your Family Group Sheets and Pedigree Charts, noting carefully where each bit of information comes from. (If you're not sure of the accuracy of something, pencil in a question mark next to that fact.)

The Sources: The Best Places to Check for Ancestors' Records

Now you're ready to search for the records your ancestors have left behind. The first place to go is to your relatives. Ask them to look for any official records they may have. Carefully look over the documents. Have you found new names? Addresses? Dates of important events? Some of this information will help you find other documents.

When you're ready to go outside the family, begin with the most common documents: vital records.

Vital Records—Birth, Marriage, and Death Certificates

Everyone is born, and everyone dies. That's one reason why birth and death certificates (vital records) are among the easiest and best places to begin searching for family documents.

Vital records often have lots of information, including hard-to-locate maiden names and addresses. Birth certificates include facts about the

Is a cemetery any place for a genealogist? Absolutely! Find out where your ancestors are buried. By reading tombstones and checking cemetery records, you may learn a great deal about your family's history.

child's parents; death certificates, filled out by relatives, often give facts about survivors.

When you start to look for your family's vital records, begin with your parents' birth and marriage certificates. Then start looking for your grandparents' documents. Move slowly backward in time.

Where to Look: Vital records are local records. They are usually kept in the capital of the county where someone lived, though some states keep them in their capital cities.

If your ancestors lived in the same state as you do, your parents may be able to tell you where to write for their records. If you're searching in another state, or if you don't know where to go, the fastest way to discover where your ancestors' vital records are is to look in a booklet called "Where to Write for Vital Records." It lists every state and explains where to find birth, marriage, divorce, and death records.

To get a copy, write to the Superintendent of Documents, U.S. Government Printing Office, Washington, DC 20402. There is a small charge. Excerpts from the 1990 edition are reprinted in the Appendix.

When you find out where the records are kept, send for them by indi-

Family plots—places where many members of the same family are buried—could be great sources of information.

cating the name of the person whose records you are looking for, and the actual or approximate date (you should at least have a year) you believe an event happened. Send a self-addressed, stamped envelope with your request. The clerk will conduct a search, and if the records exist they will be sent to you—usually after you pay a fee—within a few weeks.

Religious Records

Vital records, as important as they are, were not kept formally by many states before about 1900. If you're looking for people who lived long before that year, you may not find any government records of their birth and death.

However, there is another place that may have some of your ancestors' vital records. If you're lucky enough to know what religious institution those family members attended, there may be something of interest in their records. Many churches and synagogues kept notations about their members' births, christenings, marriages, and deaths.

Where to Look: This may take some detective work. If you know your ancestors' religious affiliation, check to see if there are any institutions of that type in the place where they lived.

If you are able to determine where your ancestor worshipped, write to the office there. Explain that you are conducting a family history search, and list the names you are researching, the dates of their lives, and the years you believe they might have belonged to the church or synagogue. "If you have any records of my ancestor, I would be most interested in seeing them. Please let me know if there is any fee." As always, enclose a self-addressed, stamped envelope.

Cemetery Records

Cemeteries are not the first place you'd think of to look for records. But if you know where your ancestors are buried, you may find a good source of family information.

Where to Look: Relatives often know where ancestors are buried. If they don't, check the individual's death certificate. These certificates generally give the name of a cemetery.

When you have located the proper cemetery, call or write to their office. Tell them you are working on a genealogical project, and explain that your ancestors are buried there. Give the ancestors' names and dates of death, and ask if the cemetery has any records that you might get copies of (or look at).

If you live nearby, you may want to go with your parents to pay a visit to the cemetery. Ask for directions, hours, and specific locations of your ancestors' graves.

The main reason to visit a cemetery is to look at tombstones. Many tombstones list genealogies, such as "Beloved father, devoted husband, cherished grandfather." Older stones frequently list several names, including infant children. Jewish tombstones usually have inscribed, in Hebrew, the name of the father of the deceased.

On just about all stones, there may be an epitaph, a few lines that tell how someone wished to be remembered. Many are straightforward: "An honest man, a loving husband" could be all you find. Others poke a little fun:

"Here lies a man of good repute
Who wore a No. 16 boot.
'Tis not recorded how he died,
But sure it is, that open wide,
The gates of heaven must have been
To let such monstrous feet within."

If you visit a cemetery, make a note of inscriptions and any decorative stonework. Take a camera, and photograph the stones.

Mark the dates on the tombstones, but absolutely do not assume they are correct without proof. Because tombstone dates were second-hand information, taken in a time of grief and difficult to correct if inaccurate, they

A death certificate is a good source for information about a person.

The census taker pays a visit in 1930. You can use old census records to fill in blanks on your family tree.

are among the most suspect of records.

When you are visiting a family grave, be sure to look over the neighboring plots. If your ancestors were immigrants, they may be buried in a fraternal organization's section of a cemetery. Other family members may also be buried nearby. Sketch out the location of the stone and its relationship to other stones of significance to your family. If you have located the grave of a distant ancestor, ask at the office who is paying the upkeep fee. You may discover a lost relative this way.

Census Forms

Every ten years since 1790, the United States has commissioned a head-count of every inhabitant of the country. The census completed in 1990 was the twenty-first in this ongoing series.

These counts take place all across the nation on one specific day determined by Congress. During the last few censuses, many people simply mailed in forms with the information required about their households. If a household did not respond, someone was sent to the home.

But in the years before mail-in

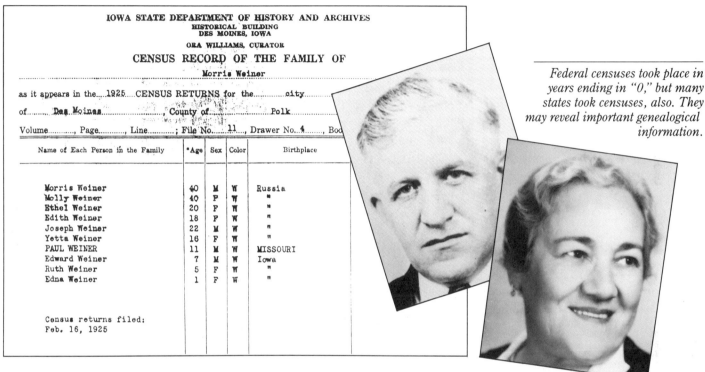

IOWA STATE DEPARTMENT OF HISTORY AND ARCHIVES
HISTORICAL BUILDING
DES MOINES, IOWA
ORA WILLIAMS, CURATOR

CENSUS RECORD OF THE FAMILY OF

Morris Weiner

as it appears in the....1925...CENSUS RETURNS for the............city............

of......Des Moines................., County of................Polk............

Volume..........., Page..........., Line...........; File No....11...., Drawer No...4....., Bod

Name of Each Person in the Family	*Age	Sex	Color	Birthplace
Morris Weiner	40	M	W	Russia
Molly Weiner	40	F	W	"
Ethel Weiner	20	F	W	"
Edith Weiner	18	F	W	"
Joseph Weiner	22	M	W	"
Yetta Weiner	16	F	W	"
PAUL WEINER	11	M	W	MISSOURI
Edward Weiner	7	M	W	Iowa
Ruth Weiner	5	F	W	"
Edna Weiner	1	F	W	"

Census returns filed:
Feb. 16, 1925

Federal censuses took place in years ending in "0," but many states took censuses, also. They may reveal important genealogical information.

forms became common, the census was a national counting party. "Census takers" or "enumerators" went door to door in every community in the United States. They didn't just count people; they also accumulated a lot of information.

If you know where your ancestor lived in any year ending in "0" from 1910 back, you can look through microfilm copies of the actual sheets of that census and discover what the census taker found out about your family.

(To protect privacy, census records are off limits to the general public for 72 years. In 1992, the 1920 census will be opened for general viewing.) When you look at a census record, you'll see—in the census taker's own handwriting—what he learned about your ancestor's home.

Census records before 1900 have less information. Until 1850, only the name of the head of household was listed. And the records of the 1890 census were lost almost completely in

a fire. In spite of all that, federal census records can be helpful. By looking up a family across two or three censuses, you can monitor changes, find out about children you never knew existed, or learn the names of children you knew about but could not identify.

Where to Look: U.S. census records are the property of the government. Copies are kept on microfilm at the National Archives in Washington, D.C., and in branch offices in 12 other cities (see "The National Archives Regional Archives System" in the Appendix). In addition, major research and genealogical libraries often have copies of the census.

To locate your ancestor in any census before 1920, ask for an index and look him or her up by state and last name. Some years are indexed alphabetically; others use the SOUNDEX system (see "Finding Your Family's Name" on page 138). Some states were not indexed, however, and you will have to know the precise address at which your ancestor lived.

You should know the name of the person who was head of the household. If you find the person you're looking for, you'll see information about their street, town, and county of residence. There will also be numbers that tell you the enumeration district, page number, and line number of the census. Write these numbers carefully; you will then have to get the proper roll of microfilm and look them up. In most places, you can make copies of them.

(Many states conducted their own censuses during off-years from federal censuses. Check with your state historical society to see if your state ever conducted its own head-counts.)

Citizenship Papers

Most immigrants, once they arrived here, wanted to become American citizens and many of them quickly filed applications. These citizenship applications are filled with information. If your family member arrived after 1906, you will probably find out from these papers what ship they arrived on and when; you may also find their photographs.

Where to Look: If your ancestors became citizens after September 26, 1906, you may track down their immigration papers by sending form G-639 to the Immigration and Naturalization Service, FOIA/PA Office, Washington, DC 20536. (You'll find a copy of this form in the Appendix; fill out and send a photocopy of it.) Tell them you want to find your ancestors' naturalization papers, and that you are applying under the Freedom of Information Act. If you don't have all the information that's required, include what you do have and send in the form anyway. There is no fee unless they find the papers.

This process may take a long time. There is a shortcut, however, *if* you know which court your ancestor was naturalized in. See if anyone has a copy of the citizenship certificate your ancestor received; that has the name of the court on it. If your ancestor lived most of his life in one county, there's a chance he was naturalized in that county's federal court.

If you find out which court handled an ancestor's naturalization, contact that court. Say you want to know how to obtain copies of your relative's naturalization papers, especially the Declaration of Intention and the Petition for Naturalization (see "Full-Fledged Americans" on the opposite page). Then either mail in your money, or do the search in person.

Be forewarned, however, that finding an ancestor's naturalization records may be very frustrating, especially if he or she applied before 1906. Up until that year, an applicant could apply at any federal, state, or local court, and the records were held *only* by the court to which he applied.

Passenger Ship Lists

A ship's manifest with your ancestors' names on it is a kind of short story. It tells you which ship they arrived on and when they arrived—and usually, a lot more. To find the ship's manifest, however, you need a great deal of information.

Full-fledged Americans: How immigrants became citizens

"I hereby declare, on oath, that I absolutely and entirely renounce and abjure all allegiance and fidelity to any state or sovereignty, and particularly to Russia or any independent state within the bounds of the former Russian empire, of whom I have heretofore been a subject; that I will support and defend the Constitution and laws of the United States against all enemies, foreign and domestic; and that I will bear true faith and allegiance to the same."

By signing that wordy pledge on June 9, 1920, my grandfather Hymie Perlo became a citizen of the United States of America.

Immigrants were not required to become American citizens, but most wanted to do so. Being a citizen meant you were a real American: You were entitled to vote in elections. You could have a say in who ran your town, your city, your state—even the country! For millions of immigrants who had no voice at all in the governing of the countries they had come from, being an American citizen was a privilege, and one they were eager to attain.

Anyone born in the United States or born to parents who are American citizens is automatically a U.S. citizen. All others must apply to be accepted for citizenship. That process is called "naturalization."

In order to become a naturalized citizen, immigrants must formally apply to do so, must learn to speak English, and must become familiar with American government and history. The procedure has changed over the years, but those standards generally have applied.

In the early 1900s, applying for citizenship was a three-step process. No sooner than three years after being legally admitted to the United States, the immigrant had to go to a federal courthouse and file a document called a "Declaration of Intention," which was sometimes called "First Papers." On this form, applicants usually gave their home addresses and information about where and when they were born, and when and how they arrived in the United States.

A year or more later, immigrants filed a second application, the "Petition for Naturalization," which was sometimes referred to as "Second Papers" or "Final Papers." On this document, immigrants repeated the information on the first papers, and may have added the name of a husband or wife and children.

Shortly thereafter, if the application was accepted (there was an investigation to ensure that there was no good reason to deny the request) the immigrant received a "Certificate of Naturalization." It was this document that the immigrant received with great pride. It meant that the immigrant was now a full-fledged U.S. citizen. Many immigrants framed or in some other way displayed their citizenship certificate.

While the certificate was the most important piece of paper as far as the immigrant was concerned, it is the Declaration and Petition that are of most use and interest to genealogists.

The first and most important piece of information is the name under which your ancestor arrived. Remember that many names—both first and last—were changed in the United States. This was especially true for eastern European immigrants with names that were long or hard-to-pronounce (for Americans, anyway).

Where to Look: Once you have the names, what you do next depends upon the date you are researching. If your ancestors came to America *before 1820*, your task may be complicated. From the 1600s until 1819, no specific government body was paying close attention to who immigrated. The only records you can count on are local ones, and finding them may require some ingenuity (see "Locating 'Early Bird' Ancestors" on page 141; for African-American ancestors, see page 134).

But if your ancestors arrived in America by ship *between 1820 and 1950*, things may be easier. Starting in 1820, the Immigration Act required ships' captains to report to the government the name, age, sex, occupation, and country of origin of each passenger. These lists contained a surprising amount of information about their passengers and fortunately, many of them

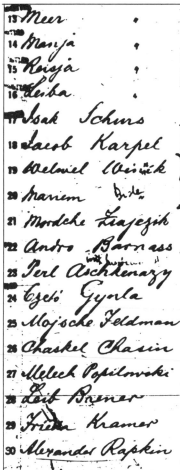

Official records may be filled with errors: Note how Alexander Rabkin's name is spelled on line 30 of this ship's manifest.

still exist today. They are stored on microfilm at the National Archives building in Washington, D.C., and in 12 branch offices around the United States (see Appendix).

The staff of the National Archives will search for the documents for you. If the only information you have is your ancestors' names, where they arrived, and the month and year of arrival, they will search their index for you and let you know the name of the ship. If you already have the name of the ship, plus the arrival names, port, and month and year, they will send you a copy of the ship's manifest. Write to the National Archives, General Reference Branch, NNRG, 8th and Pennsylvania Avenue, NW, Washington, DC 20408. Ask for the NATF Form 81. There is a small charge.

You can search yourself, of course, by going to any of the National Archives branch offices, or to one of the great genealogical libraries (see Chapter 9). If you do your own research, you do not need to know the month of arrival or the ship's name. But naturally, if you have this information, your job will be much easier.

There is always a chance you will not find your ancestors in these records. Many ships' manifests between 1820 and the early 1880s are incomplete. Some passengers were left off lists and some manifests have been lost. And if your ancestor arrived in New York City between 1847 and 1896, you may find it more difficult to locate the information; there is no overall index to those arrival documents although one is being compiled.

Military Records

Is there a family story about the heroic actions your ancestor took during a famous battle? Was great-grandpa a soldier in World War I, or did a great-great-great ancestor distinguish himself in the U.S. Civil War?

War stories turn into legends very quickly. But if anyone in your family was in the U.S. military, there are ways to verify his service. And these records may hold interesting information.

In addition to records that tell if your ancestors served in the armed forces, there are also pension records. Pension records are usually more interesting for genealogists, as they may contain facts about the pensioner after his service days: where he lived, what type of work he did, whom he married, and information about the children he had.

There are hundreds of documents that hold facts about your family, and you can get copies of many of them. This registration card, for example, was filled out by millions of American men during World War I.

Keeping dates straight: Calendar-watching for genealogists

Can someone be born three times? My grandfather was.

According to his tombstone, Morris Wolfman was born on November 16, 1879; his death certificate says November 25, 1882; and his citizenship papers say November 25, 1881.

Obviously, they can't all be correct. In fact, it's pretty obvious which date is the most reliable. The information on the tombstone and death certificate came from other people. Only the citizenship papers date came straight from my grandfather.

You will find, as you do your research, that this kind of confusion is not uncommon. While all facts in genealogy have to be checked, dates turn out to be the trickiest of all.

There are a lot of reasons for this:
• **Americans write dates differently from most other people in the world.** You probably use the American style of month-day-year. You write October 7, 1950, as 10/7/50. When you begin to look into records of other

countries, you will find that many places use a different style: day-month-year. They write 7 October 1950, or 7/10/50.

If you are not careful, you may end up wrongly assuming that 7/10/50 is July 10, not October 7. Be sure to double-check all your sources for how they make notations. The proper way to write dates for all *genealogical* research is day-month-year.

• **People were sometimes listed as younger than they really were.** For example, immigrant ship tickets for children under a certain age (sometimes 14, sometimes 12) were cheaper than adult tickets. So many parents subtracted several years from their children's ages.

Some people made themselves younger. They didn't like being 52, so they became 50. Simple—but confusing for the genealogist who follows their path. (In cases like these and the next one, the best thing to do is to look for records made closer to the time of

birth, like birth certificates or christening records.)

• **Some people made themselves *older* than they really were.** If a 16-year-old boy wanted to emigrate to America, but wasn't allowed to leave by himself until he was 18, he might figure out a way to gain two years in a hurry.

• **Some people really didn't know exactly when they were born.** No birth records were kept in many American states until after 1900. In other countries, records were often incomplete or nonexistent. And in some religions, dates were kept by a different calendar. These people were never 100 percent sure how "Tammuz" or "Ramadan" translated to our calendar, so they made something up.

• **Several countries changed their calendar.** Days disappeared and years were renumbered all around the world between 1582 and 1923 (see "The Mystery of the Missing Days" on page 136).

Was great-grandpa in the U.S. Army? His records might still exist. These Civil War soldiers came from Michigan.

Even if your ancestor did not serve in the army, if he was living in the United States between June 1917 and September 12, 1918, and was between the ages of 18 and 45 during those years, there may be some draft registration records under his name. All these records are kept by the federal government.

Where to Look: If your ancestor served in the military before 1917, check the National Archives in Washington, D.C. You must know your ancestor's full name, the approximate dates during which he served, and the state or territory from which he entered the military. If you would like the archives staff to search for your ancestor's records, send for the NATF Form 80, Order and Billing for Copies of Veterans Records. Request *all* records in your ancestor's file. Write the National Archives, Reference Services Branch, General Services Administration, Washington, DC 20408.

If you are interested in the 1917 draft registration records, write to the National Archives, Atlanta Branch, 1557 St. Joseph Avenue, East Point, GA 30344, and ask for a World War I Registration Card request form.

And if you want to search for military records after 1917, write to the

That old-time handwriting

Old documents were handwritten, and old-time script can make your eyes swim. But don't despair. If you've found an old handwritten record, you're probably looking at valuable information. It's worth taking extra time to read it carefully. Here are suggestions to make that task easier:

• **Use the known to take you to the unknown.** Study the way in which letters are crafted, particularly in obvious words. Legal documents are loaded with terms like "Whereas," and you usually can spot your ancestor's name. Make a note of the letters in those words, and try to find them in others.

• **In early American documents, be on the lookout for what is known as the "long s"** (*f*). This letter looks a lot like today's "f," but it was often used in colonial times as the first "s" when two appeared together: Congre*f*s, progre*f*s, ble*f*sing. For some good examples of this, see if you can find a copy of the handwritten Declaration of Independence.

• **Watch for common abbreviations.** Many words were shortened, with the second letter raised up. Some examples include J^r for Junior, S^d for

said, and afs^d for "the aforesaid," which means the person previously mentioned. Often names were written this way also: Abra^m stood for Abraham, W^m or Willm for William, Marg^t for Margaret.

• **Capital letters can be especially hard to figure out.** L and T often look the same; M and N, I and J, L and S, and U and V all can be difficult to differentiate. The best way to tackle any old document is to become familiar with the writer's style. Look through the document for obvious words, noting how the writer made capitals and small letters.

If you are stumped on a letter, make a list of all the letters it could possibly

be, and then search for them in the document. By process of elimination, you may be able to determine what letter you are looking at.

• **In English-language documents, read through a sentence and make guesses at what a difficult word could be.** You can sometimes fill in a missing word just by figuring out the meaning of the sentence.

• **In libraries, ask for help.** There may be a handwriting-style card for the period you are researching. At a Latter-Day Saints Family History Center, I came across a helpful full-page chart of Polish handwriting, showing a variety of styles for every letter.

National Personnel Records Center (Military Records), NARA, 9700 Page Boulevard, St. Louis, MO 63132.

Other Documents: School Records; Deeds and Other Land Records; Wills

Many other records about your ancestors exist. If you become serious about genealogy, you may find them worth exploring.

Schools keep student records for a long time; you might be able to find your great-grandmother's report card. (Imagine someone finding your own report card 100 years from now!) You can write to the schools your family members attended, give them the names and dates when they were in school, and ask if they can send you any of their records. These records can give you a peek at the younger years of your ancestors' lives.

If your family owned land, you might be able to trace the history of that land in official documents. You can find out how much the land cost, what was built on it, from whom it was bought, and to whom it was sold. You might even be able to visit it.

Most land records—often called "deeds"—are kept in the capital, or seat, of the county where the property

Alternative places to look for information

To find out a birth date, you can look at a birth certificate. But what if you can't find a birth certificate? You might try to locate a death certificate, because one of the items commonly listed on a death certificate is "date of birth."

This chart cites common bits of information that genealogists need, and suggests alternative places where you may find them. It just may help you uncover some particularly hard-to-locate facts.

WHAT YOU WANT TO FIND OUT	WHERE TO LOOK
Date of birth	Marriage license, death certificate, children's birth certificates, census records
A woman's maiden name	Her marriage or death certificate, any of her children's vital records
Children's names	Census records, wills
Date of arrival in the United States	Naturalization records
Name of ship, port of entry	Naturalization records
Line of work, business address	Local directories, census records
Family addresses	Local directories, phone books, naturalization records, vital records
Earlier ancestors' names	Birth and death records of their descendants, cemetery inscriptions
Where someone is buried	Death certificate

When land was for sale in the American West, millions responded. The records of their purchases can be found in courts across the United States. Many other settlers got their land for free; the Homestead Act of the 1860s offered a farm to anyone who worked the land for five years and became a citizen in that time.

is located. Someone in your family may have a copy of an old deed that proved an ancestor's ownership of land. If so, you can contact the office that holds the records, and ask them for more information about that land. They may discover old maps, records of sale, or other information.

You may even hear stories about an ancestor who was given land by the federal government. These "land grants" took place in 30 states, most of them in the Midwest and West. If you have reason to believe your ancestor obtained land in this way, you may want to write the National Archives for more information. Include your ancestor's full name, the state in which he or she possessed the land, and whether it was granted before or after 1908. Write to the National Archives, Reference Branch, NNRR, Washington, DC 20409.

Wills are another interesting re-source you may want to explore. These are legal documents that record what people want to have happen to their property after they die. Wills tell you what possessions and which people were important to the writer. Notice how people were referred to, and how the property was distributed. Be on the lookout for unfamiliar names— you may discover a new ancestor or two.

If you want to find an ancestor's

will, you need to know where he died and the year of his death. The best way to proceed is to contact the local civil court in the county where your ancestor died, asking if you can see a copy of that will. You should also ask about probate records. If there were questions or problems with your ancestor's will, legal hearings might have been held. Probate records are often full of valuable information.

Preserving Those Documents

These documents are more than just sources of information. They are bits of living history, snapshots of your ancestors' lives. So treat them with great care. Every time you locate a document, make a copy of it—either a photocopy or your own extract of the information. In fact, make a number of copies so you can share them with other family members.

And don't let those copies sit in a drawer, accumulating dust. One good idea is to put them in a record book, like your loose-leaf binder. Try not to cut or otherwise mark these copies; keep them safe under clear plastic sheets. After a while, you will have accumulated an ancestor scrapbook—a record of the people who make up your

heritage. That's something you can proudly share with the rest of your family.

Strategies for Special Groups

No matter what your family background is, your genealogical search is going to have special problems. Every ethnic group needs its own strategies—especially when it comes to tracking histories back to the Old

Country (see "Back to the Old Country" on page 91).

But if you are an American of African descent or a Native American Indian, you probably will face problems tracing ancestors on *this* side of the ocean. In both cases, shameful racial biases are reflected in the way the records of these groups were kept.

If you are of Jewish heritage, some strategies about getting at overseas information require special care. And if you are adopted, your research is com-

---

Checklist:
Before you go to a records center

Many record searches can be done through the mail, but sometimes you will have to go in person. Call first and ask every possible question. It is better to spend five minutes on the phone than to waste an hour going somewhere only to be told you can't use the records.

Here are the key questions to ask:
• What's your exact address? How do I get there?
• What days and what hours are you open?
• What's the latest you'll let someone

enter?
• Is there a photocopy machine there?
• If not, is there any way I can get documents copied?
• Do I need any kind of identification to look at records?
• I'm (say your age) years old. Can I look at the documents by myself?
• Do I have to pay for anything?
• Can I pay you in cash? If not, how can I pay for documents?
• Is there an information packet you could send me?
• Is there anything else I should know?

plicated by the question of confidentiality.

In all these cases, there *are* ways to find out about your heritage, and there are a number of books and organizations that will help you in your quest.

Finding Your Native American Ancestors

If you are of Native American ancestry, there are records kept by the National Archives that may be of interest to you. Much of the information relates to the so-called "Five Civilized Tribes"—the Cherokee, Chocktaw, Chickasaw, Seminole, and Cree. These tribes were forced out of their lands in the East and resettled in the Oklahoma Territory between 1830 and 1846.

Other sources worth exploring are the Latter-Day Saints Family History Library and the Oklahoma Historical Society in Oklahoma City.

A Guide to Records in the National Archives Relating to American Indians is sold by the Superintendent of Documents, U.S. Government Printing Office, Washington, DC 20402. Write for the exact price.

Finding Your African-American Ancestors

In the beginning, researching an African-American family is no different from researching any other group. As you work backward from the present, you will be taking down oral histories, filling out family charts, and searching out the same records as other Americans.

But when you arrive at the pre-Civil War era, you will probably hit a huge roadblock. Unless you are descended from one of the relatively tiny number

Some of your ancestors' history may be tinged with sorrow. In this photograph, steamboats are taking Native American Sioux Indians away from their Montana homeland.

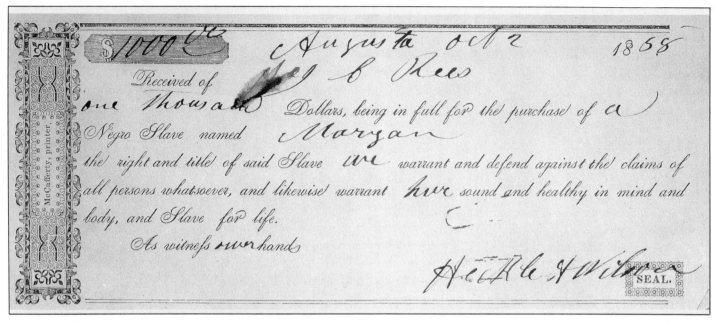

Documents can tell tragic stories—as does this 1858 receipt for the purchase "for life" of a girl named Maryan, a "Negro Slave."

of freed slaves, you will find no information about your ancestors in censuses or other records. It was not until 1870 that African-Americans were *named*, as well as counted, in the census.

It is possible, however, to find your slave ancestors. Among the many who have done this are *Roots* author Alex Haley, tennis player Arthur Ashe, TV star Bill Cosby, and Dorothy Spruill Redford, co-author of a stirring 1988 book about her search called *Somerset Homecoming*.

The best starting point is a book entitled *Black Genesis: An Annotated Bibliography for Black Genealogical Research,* edited by James M. Rose and Alice Eichholz. Two other helpful books are *Black Genealogy,* by Charles L. Blockson and Ron Fry, and *Slave Genealogy: A Research Guide with Case Studies,* by David H. Streets.

There are special records in the National Archives about African-Americans who served in the military from the 1860s on. The archives and the Mormon (Latter-Day Saints)

branch libraries are the major holders of records relating to African-American genealogy.

Finding Your Eastern European Jewish Ancestors

The special problems of Jewish research occur on the other side of the ocean. Most Jewish immigrants came from eastern Europe between 1880 and 1924. Nearly all of the communities those immigrants came from were destroyed, and the inhabitants murdered, by the Nazis during the Holocaust and World War II.

But while the communities were destroyed, many records were not. In fact, an astonishing number of documents survived. Many have been photographed and placed on microfilm by the Church of Jesus Christ of Latter-Day Saints.

In addition, there are memorial books to hundreds of these communities. Called *Yizkor* books, they include photographs, reminiscences, and obituaries for many of the people killed between 1938 and 1945. These books, which often have a section in English, can be found in libraries with large collections of Judaica, such as the YIVO Institute in New York City, the

The mystery of the missing days

In 1752, something very odd happened in the British Isles and all English colonies, including America. Eleven days—September 3 through 13—disappeared. People went to sleep on September 2, 1752. When they woke up the next morning, the date was September 14, 1752.

These are the famous "missing days" that keep genealogists on their toes. They vanished in British lands in 1752, but a number of days have disappeared in other countries, too, at other times.

As a result of this mystery, you may find dates in the 18th century written with two numbers:

11 Feb. 1731 O.S. / 22 Feb. 1732 N.S.

Here's how it happened: The British were among the last people in the world to accept the fact that the calendar they were using was flawed. The "Julian" calendar—named after Julius Caesar,

who adopted it around 45 B.C.—called March 25 New Year's Day, and said the year was 365 days and 6 hours long. The length was very close—only wrong by a few minutes. But after nearly 2,000 years, those few minutes added up to an error of 10 days. Most of the world adopted a new calendar (advocated by Pope Gregory XIII), called the "Gregorian" calendar, sometime after 1582, when they jumped forward by 10 days and October 5 became October 15.

The British refused to go along until the middle of the 18th century, and by then, the difference had grown to 11 days. Finally, on September 2, 1752, the British joined most of the world and changed their calendar. In all British lands (with the exception of Scotland, which had changed 100 years before), September 2 was followed by September 14. And 1753 began on January 1,

not on March 25.

All this means is that you have to double-check the dates you find in English-speaking countries between 1582 and 1752. Are they listed as O.S. (Old Style) or N.S. (New Style)? Do you see a date listed 1750/51? That would probably be a date between January 1 and March 24—which means that 1750 is the old-style notation and 1751 is the one we now use.

Here is when the date changes took place in some other countries:
Austria: January 7, 1584, became January 17, 1584
France: December 10, 1582, became December 20, 1582
Norway: February 19, 1700, became March 1, 1700
Sweden: February 18, 1753, became March 1, 1753

Family history often connects with world history. For many Jewish genealogists, the giant shadow of the Holocaust—the death of six million Jews at the hands of the Nazis during World War II—becomes far darker when they discover how many of their own ancestors were killed. Above, cousins of Max Burstein, all of whom died in the Holocaust.

New York Public Library, and the collections of the Jewish Historical Society in Waltham, Massachusetts.

If You Were Adopted

Adopted children generally cannot find out about their birth parents until they turn 18. There is an organization, the Adoptees Liberty Movement Association (ALMA), that will help you attempt to trace your history. But they will not work with anyone under 18.

ALMA has an Adoption Reunion Registry with 700,000 names of adoptive parents and children who are seeking each other. If you wish information about them, write ALMA, P.O. Box 154, Washington Bridge Station, New York, NY 10033.

As an adopted child, there is one heritage you *can* easily trace before you're 18: that of your adoptive family. Your parents have carried forward the gifts and traditions of their families, and by tracing their heritage you will learn a great deal about them—and about yourself, too.

Finding your family's name: Using the sounds of SOUNDEX

As you search for your ancestors' records, you will discover a very confusing fact: Your family name, or surname, can be spelled many different ways.

Your grandfather's surname may be Smith, Smyth, and Smythe on three different documents. Two brothers may spell their surnames differently: one named Li, the other Lee. Even simple surnames such as Jones can be spelled a dozen ways (Joans, Jhones, Jonnes, etc).

There are a number of reasons why there is so much confusion about surnames. For many years, names were not standardized. Sometimes people didn't know how to write, so officials interviewing them made up letters to fit what they heard. Other times, the individual wasn't consistent in the way he spelled his own name. Finally, many people changed the spelling of their names to fit the country they were in.

These changeable names can make your research difficult. That is one reason why the U.S. government adopted a special indexing code called SOUNDEX.

Under the SOUNDEX system, names are grouped together by sound rather than letter, which makes it possible to find names with the same sound—no matter how they are spelled. You'll discover that many immigration records, some U.S. Census records, and a lot of other documents are indexed by SOUNDEX.

Every SOUNDEX code has a letter and *three* numbers. The first letter of SOUNDEX is always the same as the first letter in the surname. For example, people named Fedelovich, no matter what spelling they used (like Faitelovicz, Foodelovich, or Feydalovich) could find their records under the heading F341.

Note: If your name was substantially changed or shortened after arrival in the United States, you should find out what the *original* name was when searching early records, because if you're looking under Aggins but the original name was Agaranowisinski, you won't find anything.

Before you search, you should figure out your SOUNDEX code. Here's how you do it.

1. Let's take the name Johannson. The first letter of the name always remains the same. So the first SOUNDEX space in this case is filled with J.

NAME: J O H A N N S O N
SOUNDEX: J _ _ _

2. Now look at the SOUNDEX code:

Letter	Number
B P F V	1
C S K G J Q X Z	2
D T	3
L	4
M N	5
R	6

Ignore the letters A, E, I, O, U, W, Y, and H.

3. Go through the name, crossing out those letters SOUNDEX tells you to ignore:

NAME: J Ø H̸ A̸ N N S Ø N

4. If you have any double letters, treat them as one letter. For the NN in Johannson, for example, cross out one N.

NAME: J Ø H̸ A̸ N̸ N S Ø N

5. Finally, fill in the other three SOUNDEX spaces with the numbers that represent the remaining letters:

NAME: J Ø H̸ A̸ N̸ N S Ø N
SOUNDEX: J 5 2 5

6. No matter how many letters there are in the name, every SOUNDEX code is made up of one letter and three numbers. So, J 525 is the number you will use to look through the SOUNDEX index for the name Johannson. This code would also work for Johanson, Johnson, and Johnsson, among other names.

7. If different letters that are side by side have the same number—as they would in JACKSON (C, K and S are all number 2)—use the number only once.

8. Every SOUNDEX code must have one letter and three numbers. If your name code ends up shorter than that, you must add zeroes to the code. For example, Lee, which translates to L, would become L000.

9. If there is a prefix in your name—such as van der Horst or de Mornay—figure out your SOUNDEX code both with and without it. Try "Mornay" and "deMornay." Your documents may be filed under either name. (MAC and MC are *not* considered prefixes, so those names will be coded only as M _ _ _ .)

10. Finally, here's how you use the index. If you are looking up Johannson, you will go to the J525 names, and begin searching alphabetically by *first name*. In other words, Alice Johnson will be listed among the first J525s. Zachary Johanson will be among the last J525s.
Now spell out your own name:

— — — — — — — — — — — —

And code it into SOUNDEX:

— — — —

Double-check your results. It's important to be sure you've got the right code. Now you're ready to look through federal SOUNDEX indexes.

Here are some other names in SOUNDEX:

R Ø G E̸ R S	R262
L E̸ W̸ I̸ S	L200
R U̸ S S̸ E̸ L L̸	R240
K Ø V̸ A̸ L C H̸ I̸ C K	K142

CHAPTER NINE

You Could Look It Up

Libraries and Other Resources

There's one great genealogical resource we haven't talked about yet: libraries. Whether big or small, libraries have maps, directories, local histories, even published genealogies—all of which can help you in your research.

The key to getting the most out of any library is to know what's in it. This is as true of your small local branch as it is of the biggest libraries in the world.

Local Libraries

Let's say your great-grandparents lived in the same town as you do now, and you are looking for details of their lives. Visit your local library and tell the librarian, "I'm doing research on

my family's life in this town in the 1880s and 1890s." Then politely ask some questions:

• Is there a local history section? What kind of materials does it have? Are there newspaper clippings? Old phone or city directories? Business listings? Local maps? Family histories?

• What kind of indexes or card catalogs will help me use the materials?

• Do you have any special materials that are helpful to people doing family history research?

• Does the library have any indexes to larger genealogical collections?

Books of general interest to genealogists are filed under call number 929.1 in the Dewey decimal code. You may want to browse through that section to see if anything interests you. You should also look at genealogical magazines and newsletters if the library subscribes to them.

But your major interest here is in local materials. You might find a history of your town or county that was written to commemorate the community's special anniversary. Check the index; your ancestors or their businesses may be mentioned. Or maybe there's some information about schools they attended, or an event you've heard about at family get-

Locating "early bird" ancestors

An early view of Boston Harbor.

Passenger lists before 1820 are not in the National Archives except for a small, incomplete collection for the port of Philadelphia. But they may be on file at the actual port of entry or in the archives of the state where the port is located.

If you know where your ancestor arrived in America before 1820, begin your search by examining some of the many guides to records of those years. Two starting points are *Passenger and Immigration List Index: A Guide to Published Arrival Records*, by P. William Filby, and *A Bibliography of Ship Passenger Lists, 1583–1825*, by Harold Lancour. Your local library may either have these publications or be able to help you find copies.

Many colonial and U.S. ports kept copies of manifests filed as a requirement of clearance. These records are incomplete and rarely indexed, but are helpful when there are no other records.

Many ships' logs have been collected by museums across the United States. Some of the more notable collections are at: U.S. Mariner's Museum, Newport News, Virginia; Mystic Seaport, Mystic, Connecticut; National Maritime Museum, San Francisco, California; Newport Historical Society, Newport, Rhode Island; Peabody Museum, Salem, Massachusetts; Great Lakes Historical Society, Vermillion, Ohio; Great Lakes Maritime Museum, Detroit, Michigan; Bernice P. Bishop Museum, Honolulu, Hawaii.

If your ancestors entered at any of these ports, it may be worthwhile to examine these logs. This is especially true if you know the name of the boat they arrived on.

Two books to help you find an ancestor's ship

When did your ancestor's ship arrive in the United States? What did it look like? Once you know the name of the ship, there are two books that can help you answer those questions.

The first is the *Morton Allan Directory of European Passenger Steamship Arrivals*. This book, carried in almost every genealogical library in the United States, lists the dates of passenger ship arrivals in New York, Philadelphia, Boston, and Baltimore.

The book is arranged by port and year. Look up the *Ryandam*, 1909, coming into New York City, and within minutes you will find every date on which the ship came into that port.

If you'd like to see what your ancestor's ship looked like, try to find *Ships of Our Ancestors*, compiled by Michael J. Anuta. It's filled with small photographs of vessels that brought immigrants over. There is also a short list of facts about the ships—their tonnage, the year they were built, who owned them, and so on. This book is also carried by many genealogical libraries.

togethers. Even if you don't find anything personal, these histories are worth a glance for local color.

Speaking of local color, you should definitely look for a collection of local newspapers. In addition to town news, you might find information about your family members in the birth, wedding, or death announcements. (If you know when someone in your family was married, for example, check two or three days after the event took place.)

Old local directories can be a very valuable resource. They were like telephone books, except almost no one had a phone before about 1910. These books listed everyone—or nearly everyone—who lived in town, and included business addresses and often home addresses. The directories were published as far back as the early 1800s in some cities and towns. If you find one, check for your ancestors' addresses. Old phone books can be helpful in the same way, giving you more addresses for your records.

Finding an address may—in the great tradition of genealogical hunting—lead you to more information: If the library has old town maps, you may be able to find your ancestors' homes on one of them.

If you find something of interest,

don't just scribble it down. Write legibly and with care. Probably the greatest frustration researchers have is trying to read their own handwriting a few weeks later. Also be sure to make a clear note of where you find information. Write down the library you are in, the complete title of the book, its author, its date of publication, and the page number.

If there's a call number on the book, write that down, too. Whenever you photocopy a page, note all the source information on the back—it's very easy to forget which book a page comes from.

As for those indexes to larger collections: Check them out. If you find anything of interest, ask your librarian how you would best go about getting the materials. Your branch may be able to borrow books for you through interlibrary loan programs.

Historical and Genealogical Libraries

You may find your town has a historical society, or even a genealogical society, with a library. These places have many more books on local history, but be careful. It's easy to get lost and waste time in big libraries if you don't narrow

The National Archives building in Washington, D.C., is often called "The Nation's Attic." Millions of documents are preserved inside.

down your search. Before you wander into such a library, determine what it is you want to find. Then call ahead and see if the library can help you.

These libraries may have hundreds of family histories, complete collections of local publications (including directories, local histories, etc.), local vital records, books of passenger arrival lists, and/or old census records.

The indexes, card catalogs, and other research aids are even more important here than in smaller libraries. If you have any questions about how to use them, ask the librarian for help.

The Greatest Genealogical Library in the World

There is one place every genealogist turns to eventually: the Family History Library in Salt Lake City, Utah. This giant records center has more genealogical documents than any library on earth. It even has copies of records more than 700 years old!

The library is run by the Church of Jesus Christ of Latter-Day Saints (LDS), otherwise known as the Mormons, but the materials in it are open to the public, free of charge.

Best of all, you can get to much of this information without leaving your

Genealogical libraries can be great places for Ancestor Detectors—if they're prepared. It's best to call ahead, and go looking for something specific.

home state because the LDS also runs 1,250 branches of the Family History Library. They are found across the United States and in 43 other countries. At these branches, called Family History Centers, you can order copies of the records kept in Salt Lake City. They will be sent to the local branch, where you can use them for months on end at a minimal charge.

The LDS libraries have extraordinary microfilmed records. You can find millions of copies of documents from the United States, including every census through 1910, immigrant arrival records, wills, probate records, records from many religious institutions, and birth, marriage, and death records prior to 1900.

The Family History Centers also have access to copies of records from just about every European country, plus records from Asia, Africa, Australia, and South America.

The list of materials available goes on and on: nearly 200,000 books about genealogy; a computer database (the International Genealogical Index) that includes names and information on 100 million deceased people; research aids like translation and handwriting guides.

To find the Family History Center nearest you, look in the White Pages under "Church of Jesus Christ of Latter-Day Saints," or write to the Family History Library, 35 North West Temple Street, Salt Lake City, UT 84150, and ask for a list of the centers in your area.

The main reason the Latter-Day Saints have done all this is that genealogy is a part of their religion. Mormons believe that by locating their ancestors, they can save their souls and reunite them with their families after death. It is fortunate for the rest of the world's genealogists that they have been willing to share their findings.

Other Great Libraries

Here are 14 other American libraries that have big, important genealogical collections.

California: Los Angeles Public Library, 630 West Fifth Street, Los Angeles, CA 90071

District of Columbia: Library of Congress, Thomas Jefferson Building, 10 First Street, SE, Washington, DC 20540 / Library, National Society of the Daughters of the American Revolution, 1776 D Street, NW, Washington, DC 20006

Illinois: Newberry Library, 60 West Walton Street, Chicago, IL 60610

Indiana: Allen County Public Library, 900 Webster Street, Fort Wayne, IN 46802

Maryland: The George Peabody Library of the Johns Hopkins University, 17 East Mount Vernon Place, Baltimore, MD 21202

Massachusetts: New England Historic Genealogical Society, 101 Newbury Street, Boston, MA 02116

Michigan: Burton Collection, Detroit Public Library, 5201 Woodward Avenue, Detroit, MI 48202

New York: New York Public Library, Fifth Avenue and 42nd Street, New York, NY 10018 / New York Genealogical & Biographical Society, 122 East 58 Street, New York, NY 10022

Ohio: Western Reserve Historical Society, 10825 East Boulevard, Cleveland, OH 44106

Texas: Dallas Public Library, 1515 Young Street, Dallas, TX 75201

Virginia: National Genealogical Society Library, 4527 17 Street N, Arlington, VA 22207

Wisconsin: State Historical Society of Wisconsin, 816 State Street, Madison, WI 53706

CHAPTER TEN

Sharing the Wealth

HOW TO HELP OTHERS ENJOY YOUR GENEALOGICAL DISCOVERIES

Share your research! This is an important rule for Ancestor Detectors. Genealogy isn't only about the past; it should enlighten people in the present and preserve both past and present for the future.

It's important, therefore, that you don't leave all the information you've uncovered sitting in a file drawer or loose-leaf notebook. Spread your knowledge around. Let your relatives in on all the wonderful things you've learned. By doing this, you will spread joy *and* get back information to help you continue your research.

There are a number of ways to

Somewhere in Minnesota in 1905, members of this family posed in their Sunday best. What stories do your old family photos tell?

share the wealth: creating a family display book; putting out a newsletter; creating and distributing a master list of family names and addresses; helping put together a family reunion; forming a family club; even publishing a book about your family. All of these projects require help from an adult, although some are simpler than others. Tackle the one that suits you best, or make up one of your own.

Family Show: Display Books

After you've done some research, you'll probably have a small collection of family documents, maps, and photos. One of the easiest ways to share your findings is to put them together in a family display book.

A loose-leaf notebook and some clear plastic display pages—sold in stationery and art-supply stores—will make a fine display book. Gather all your copies of documents: birth, marriage, and death certificates, immigration papers, passenger ship lists, etc. Also include maps of your family's hometown, showing the places where they've lived, old letters, and family photographs. Then arrange each set of papers by family. Put them in the display pages, beginning with the oldest documents and moving to the newest. In that way, you'll be able to leaf through the pages and see your family's history develop.

Keep adding documents as you find them, and show your book to relatives. It will be fun to share your discoveries—and it may even inspire other family members to help you with your research.

Drop Me a Line: Family Newsletters

A newsletter does not have to be fancy. All you need is a typewriter and access to a photocopying machine. You can begin with a one-page typed sheet of information, as long is it is topped with a design, title, or name that indicates that this is the family paper, edited by you. Family newsletters typ-

ically come out one, two, or three times a year.

Your title can be as simple or as fanciful as you like. Charlotte Fox Rogers, a genealogist in Pennsylvania, edits a newsletter called "GAMSU," after the family name of her ancestors. A more unusual approach was taken by members of the Aronheim family, whose newsletter in the 1890s went by the rather striking name of "The

One of the wonderful things about family reunions is that they can be fancy affairs or simple parties. Some reunions take place in hotels, with relatives flying in from all over the world. Others are friendly backyard gatherings, like the 1981 Wolfman reunion pictured below, which featured barbecue, kids playing games, and lots of family stories.

Family reunions give children a chance to make new friends.

Occasional Booze."

A newsletter is the perfect place for family news—births, weddings, and deaths, as well as graduations, christenings, confirmations, bar and bat mitzvahs, family relocations, and other special events. A copy of the family tree would interest readers, as would photocopies of pictures you've discovered, or old documents like a ship's manifest with an ancestor's name on it. You might include profiles of interesting family members, art work, summaries of research, and jokes.

The lifeline of any newsletter is the reaction of its readers. Encourage your subscribers to send you notes, announcements, stories, drawings, and photographs. With a little bit of help from friendly relatives, you may find yourself a big-time family publisher.

A Roster of Relatives: Master Lists

If you don't have time for a newsletter, consider mailing out a master list of names and addresses. As family historian, you become a connecting point for a lot of people who don't know each other. By sending out a list with names and current addresses—information you accumulate while doing your genealogy research—you may put people in touch with each other. You can also ask your readers to add any names and addresses you may be missing.

This is a small gesture, but it comes in very handy if you ever try to help organize a family reunion.

Gather Round: The Fun of Family Reunions

One of the liveliest ways to share and celebrate your common heritage is to attend a family reunion.

What could be more entertaining, or exciting, or *fun* than a great gathering of all your relatives? Visits from family no one has seen in years. Sharing and laughing and eating and singing.

"Anyone who holds a family reunion has got to be crazy," says Eileen Lyons Polakoff, a New York City genealogist who, with her husband Jack, organized the first Schwartz-Bisgeier-Polakoff reunion in 1986 (145 people attended). "It's an enormous amount of hard work, and you'll end up doing all of it."

But even though she remembers how time-consuming it was, Eileen says it was worth it. "You create a very special connection for people at a family reunion," she says. "Older relatives get to relive a part of their life when they see family they haven't seen in years. For younger people, it's a kind of proof: 'Hey, I've got a past. I've got something to connect to.' And for kids, it's a great opportunity to make friends and play with relatives their own age."

Reunions can be anything from a small gathering at your family's house to a giant party at a football stadium. At the first reunion that Cecelia Kailaa Freeman organized for her family in Hawaii, about 50 people showed up. But after 13 years of reunions, the Kauaua clan's party in 1988 attracted 5,000 relatives! "Our family reunions have created one unit out of many, many strangers," says Hoaliku Drake, one of Cecelia's nieces. "They have been a wonderful force for good."

Obviously, you don't have to have thousands of relatives in order to have a reunion. Small reunions can be as much fun as big ones. Here are some pointers to help you put together a reunion.

- **Plan in advance.** Even a small party requires a lot of notice. Pick the date and the place well in advance, aiming for convenience for other family members (summer weekends are often a good bet). Three to six months is best; that gives you time to recruit other family members to help. And whatever date you choose, remember that it is 100 percent impossible to pick a date that will satisfy everyone.

- **Mail out a packet of information.** The invitation should be creative, promising a special family gathering, and maybe including a list of the people you've invited. Ask people to tell you if they'd be interested in attending, and if they know of other family members who should attend. It's also a good idea to ask relatives if they have any photographs or other memorabilia that they could send ahead so you can prepare it for viewing by all the family.

Remember that it will cost money to run the reunion. You have to pay for mailings and phone calls, feed everybody, and maybe even hire a hall or provide entertainment. Discuss with your parents how you want to handle this. Many family reunions have some kind of price per person to cover food, drink, and other costs.

- **Plan events for the party.** Most reunion time is spent sitting and talking, but it's nice to have a few events planned. You could have a recitation of the family history, a few speeches from the family elders, or a fun event like a dance contest.

The Galloway clan of North Carolina, Philadelphia, and other points east and south is descended from a slave named William Henry Brinkley. The Galloways have held reunions at a different family location every year since 1969. In 1988, the New Jersey branch hosted 150 guests. They sponsored a dinner at a local hotel. All entertainment was provided by family members. A raffle, dancing to records, a family talent show, a limbo contest, and a mother-daughter fashion show topped the bill.

A speech of general welcome was given and then Rosa Galloway, the family historian, recited the entire six-generation family tree. The event was videotaped, and copies were made for those who wanted to buy one.

Reunions don't have to be formal. A Wolfman family reunion was a barbecue in cousin Michael's backyard. The entertainment consisted of conversation, kids chasing each other around the yard, and the Wolfman brothers reciting the family's old phone numbers. A great time was had by all!

- **Get everything in place as the event draws near.** When the reunion is just a few weeks away, send out a one-page reminder, or call relatives

At the Polakoff family reunion, relatives stared at their giant family tree, trying to find their names on the huge chart of ancestors. At these get-togethers, old friends reunite and new friendships are made.

who said they might come. "This is one of the best times to ask for information," says Eileen Polakoff. "No one wants wrong information published about them."

Be sure that all your materials are ready. Name tags are important; you could color-code them so everyone knows which side of the family everyone else is from. Mount documents like marriage licenses, high-school diplomas, and maps of the old neighborhood or town.

Old photographs are probably the most popular of all attractions. Mount them (use copies when possible) carefully, and identify as many people, dates, and places as you can. If you've got photos you can't identify, mount them and ask, "Who is this?" underneath. You might even create a "wanted" poster of relatives you can't identify or those you've lost contact with. Leave room for people to write down information.

● **Family trees are a must.** At the Schwartz reunion, Eileen had a huge family tree—with more than 800 names!—prominently posted and covered in clear plastic. This allowed people to study their branches and make corrections or additions.

Have an evaluation sheet at the reunion. This will allow everyone who attends to get in their two cents and tell you what worked and what didn't. It also can let you know who'd be willing to work with you on other family projects.

All Join In: A Family Club

In spite of all the hard work, one family reunion usually inspires another. These events remind people of how much they have in common, and they usually want at least one more chance to share before they lose touch again. (And there are many cases in which families become closer, and stay closer, as a result of a reunion.)

"What tends to happen," says *Roots* author Alex Haley, "is that the first little group is chuckled at by other family members. 'Ha, imagine, a family reunion.' But when they hear about the good time had by the first group, they end up going to the second one. Something starts to take hold in these people, and once they gather again, they turn into something bigger than a family—they become a clan. A sense of soul, of *us*, starts to develop."

One way to keep the family in touch is to start a club or family association. The group may simply agree to get together on holidays, or to send cards out to each other. They may sponsor family research, or plan out the next family reunion.

Some families go beyond the purely social and turn into true organizations that charge dues and hire an accountant to keep track of their money. "I know of families in which this kind of organization leads to a fund to help the younger people," says Alex Haley. "In fact, I know of one black family that had such a fund, and one member of that family had an idea in which he believed. The family fund lent him $700 back about 30 years ago," Haley recalls. "His name is Berry Gordy, and the idea he had such faith in back then was a record company called Motown." It went on to be a gigantic success, making Gordy a multi-millionaire— money he might never have made without his family club's help.

Family Bestsellers: Preserve Your History

After you've done a lot of research, you might consider assembling all the information into a "compiled genealogy," or family book.

You could type it up and make photocopies, then bind them in a looseleaf or other simple binder.

Try to include the following:
- An introduction that explains which families are covered. A good place to begin is with your furthest-back ancestors, telling who they were, what you know about them, and who their descendants were.
- A history that follows the generations from the past forward. Descriptions of your ancestors' towns, their occupations, any details about their lives. Profiles of the more interesting or colorful people in your family. There is a place for family folklore here, but be sure to label a story "a family myth" or "legend" if you cannot prove it really happened.
- A description of how your family came to this country.
- A family tree, listing everyone you have found and whatever details you may have (dates and places).
- Any photographs, documents, or maps that help tell your story.
- An index listing the pages on which each ancestor's name can be found.
- A family roster.
- A source list, telling where your

information comes from (makes your book more authoritative).

There is one crucial rule: Be accurate. If you do not know which date is right, or if you are not sure of any fact, make that clear in the book. There's nothing wrong with including questionable information, as long as it is *clearly labeled* as such. But passing down misinformation is a disservice to everyone.

At the beginning of your research, you should check to see if anyone else has written a book about a branch of your family. Ask your local librarians if they know where you can locate one of the many catalogs that include lists of published family histories. (And ask them about *Genealogies in the Library of Congress: A Bibliography*, and its supplements, edited by Marion J. Kaminkow.) If one has been done on your family, try—through interlibrary loan or other means—to read through it. It may save you time and give you information you haven't seen before. Just double-check the facts; many compiled histories, especially early ones, are known to have been inaccurate in places.

When you have finished writing your story, have someone read it over for grammatical and typographical errors. If you're going to share this with your family members—and with the future—you want it to be correct and readable. Typos that change Jan into Jane or Tate into Tote will drive everyone crazy years from now.

Family books make wonderful gifts at reunions or holiday time. No matter how small your book is, relatives will be pleased to receive it. (Some people ask for a small contribution to cover costs; that's up to you.)

Don't assume that no one else is interested in your family besides your family, however. If your history is substantial—carefully researched, and more than 60 or 70 pages—you should consider contacting your local library and offering them a copy. In fact, you should even write the Library of Congress and suggest you send them one to add to their collection of compiled genealogies. Write to the Library of Congress, Genealogy Division, Washington, DC 20540.

Your future will thank you.

Before you know it, little children grow up and "today" turns into "long ago." As a family historian, you are doing something very special—preserving all the yesterdays and todays for tomorrow.

Appendix

A Dictionary of American Last Names

The following list includes translations and origins of almost 400 family names found in the United States. American family names come from all nationalities and cultures—so this list is made up of names from every part of the earth. Much of the information is adapted from a wonderful book, *The New Dictionary of American Family Names,* by Elsdon C. Smith.

The following code is used to explain the origin of the names:

(Ar) Arabic
(Arm) Armenian
(Chi) Chinese
(Cz) Czech
(Cz-Sl) Czecho-Slovakian
(Dan) Danish
(Du) Dutch
(Eng) English
(Est) Estonian
(Fin) Finnish
(Fr) French
(Ger) German
(Heb) Hebrew
(Hin) Hindi
(Hun) Hungarian
(Ir) Irish
(It) Italian
(Jap) Japanese
(Kor) Korean
(Mx) Manx
(Nor) Norwegian
(Pol) Polish
(Port) Portuguese
(Rus) Russian
(Scot) Scottish
(Sl) Slovakian
(Sp) Spanish
(Swe) Swedish
(Swi) Swiss
(Ukr) Ukrainian
(Wel) Welsh

Ackroyd *(Eng)* Dweller at the oak clearing

Adler *(Ger)* Dweller at the sign of the eagle

Altman *(Ger)* Old man

Armstrong *(Eng)* One who was noted for his strength

Arzt *(Ger)* Doctor

Bader *(Ger)* Barber

Ballard *(Eng)* The bald one

Barkan *(Heb)* Son of a Cohen (priest)

Bauer *(Ger)* Farmer (also Bauman, Baumann)

Baxter *(Eng)* Baker (female)

Becker *(Ger)* Baker

Beebe *(Eng)* Dweller on a bee farm

Belcher *(Fr)* Beautiful, beloved

Bell *(Eng)* Dweller at the sign of the bell

Berra *(It)* Dweller in a hut

Bevilaqua *(It)* Teetotaler, one who drinks only water

Bialik *(Sl)* The white-haired one

Black *(Eng)* The dark-haired one

Bleecker *(Du)* One who bleaches clothing

Bogart *(Du)* Worker in an orchard

Boggs *(Eng)* Dweller in a marsh

Borg *(Ger, Swe, Nor)* Dweller in or near a fortified castle

Bouvier *(Fr)* One who took care of cattle

Bradley *(Eng)* Inhabitant of a broad pastureland (brad-lee); (similarly Bradstreet. Bradhurst, Bradford)

Brenner *(Ger)* Distiller

Breuer *(Ger)* Brewer (also Brewer, Brewster, Brower)

Brody *(Ger)* A place name

Buick *(Du)* One who had a large stomach or paunch

Bullwinkel *(Ger)* Dweller at the corner where bulls were kept

Bumstead *(Eng)* Dweller from Bumpstead (a reedy place) in Essex

Buren *(Du)* Dweller in the neighborhood

Cabot *(Fr)* One with a small head

Caputo *(It)* One with a large or unusual head; stubborn or dull-witted

Carpenter, Carpentier *(Eng, Fr)* One who worked with wood

Carson *(Scot, Eng, Mx)* Dweller at or near a marsh; also garçon or servant; or son of Car, short for Carmichael

Chevrolet *(Fr)* Dweller at the sign of the little goat

Cleaver *(Eng)* Dweller near a cliff

Cloud *(Scot)* Dweller near the rock or mass of stone; son of Leod

Cooper *(Eng)* Barrel maker

Copple *(Eng)* One who came from Copple (peaked hill) in Lancashire; or from Cople (Cocca's pool) in Bedfordshire

Corona *(It)* One who played the king's part in pageants and festivals; dweller at the sign of the crown

Crawford *(Eng)* One who came from Crawford (crow's pass) in Lanarkshire; dweller near a river crossing where crows are

Crocker *(Eng)* Someone who makes pots (crockery)

Crockett *(Eng)* Little, crooked, or deformed person

Cronkite *(Ger, Du)* One who was ill, an invalid, American corruption of Krankheit

Cullen *(Ger)* From Koln, Cologne

Currier *(Eng)* One who dressed, or prepared, leather

Czyz *(Pol)* Dweller at the sign of the yellow or green finch; finchlike

Dannenberg *(Ger)* One who came from town of Dannenberg (which means pine-tree-covered mountain), the name of three places in Germany

Desai *(Hin)* District officer, descendant of Desai, Hindi title with no English equivalent

Dick *(Ger, Eng)* Large, fat man; descendant of Dick, pet form of Richard

Diener *(Ger)* Server

Disney *(Eng)* One who comes from Isigny (Isina's estate) in Calvados

Dombrowski *(Pol)* Dweller in or near the oak grove

Doolittle *(Fr, Eng)* One who lived *de l'hôtel*, in the mansion; an idler

Douglas *(Eng)* Dweller at the black water or stream; one who came from Douglas in Lancashire

Dresner *(Ger)* From Dresden

Dreyfuss *(Fr)* One who came from Treves, in France

Duchin *(Heb)* One who gave the priestly blessing

Farber *(Ger)* Painter

Fisch *(Ger)* Fisherman, one who dwelt at the sign of the fish

Fleischer *(Ger)* Butcher

Ford, Forde, Forder *(Eng)* Dweller or worker at a stream crossing

Fowler *(Eng)* Bird catcher or gamekeeper

Frank *(Ger)* One who came from Franconia

Fu *(Chi)* Teacher

Gabler *(Eng)* Tax collector

Gebauer *(Ger)* Peasant or tiller of the fields

Gerber *(Ger)* Tanner

Gillick *(Ir)* The son of Ulick, a pet form of William (resolution, helmet)

Grant *(Eng, Fr, Scot)* Large or fat man

Griffin *(Eng)* Dweller at the sign of the half-lion half-eagle; also one with a ruddy complexion

Hallas *(Pol)* Noisy, bustling man

Hallmark *(Eng)* Nickname, half-a-mark, that is, one-third of a pound, possibly for one who paid a coin of that denomination annually as rent for his land; dweller on, or near, the hill field

Halpern, Halperin *(Heb, Ger)* Money changer; one who came from Heilbronn (holy well) in Wurtemberg

Hooper, Hoopes *(Eng)* One who made hoops, a cooper; one who lived on the hop, a piece of enclosed land in a marsh

Horowitz *(Cz-Sl, Rus)* One who came from Horice or Horitz (mountainous place) in Bohemia; son of the mountaineer

Horvath, Horvat *(Hun)* One who came from Croatia

Jaffee *(Heb)* Pretty

Kaczmarek, Kaczmarski *(Pol)* Descendant of the bartender

Kefauver *(Ger)* Maker of javelins or spears

Keller *(Fr, Eng, Ger)* One employed in a storeroom, particularly a food storage place; one who made or sold culs or kells, a cap or hairnet for women; one who came from Keller (wine cellar), several places in Germany

Kellerman *(Ger)* Worker, or dweller, in a wine cellar or tavern

Kessler *(Ger)* Coppersmith, one who sold or made kettles. Jewish Kesslers get their name not from a profession but from the Hebrew name of an ancestor called "Yekutiel," whose nickname was Kessel; Kessler means "one descended from Kessel"

Kim *(Kor)* Gold

Kite *(Eng)* Dweller at the sign of the kite or hawk

Klein *(Ger)* The short man

Klutz *(Ger)* One who came from Klutz (hot, bubbling spring) in Germany

Kosek *(Pol)* Dweller at the sign of the little blackbird

Koski, Koskinen *(Finn)* Dweller at the rapids or near a waterfall

Kramer *(Ger)* Merchant

Kravitz, Kravetz, Kravets, Kravits *(Cz-Sl, Pol, Ukr)* One who made outer garments, a tailor

Krieger *(Ger)* Warrior; Yiddish could mean tavern keeper

Kumamoto *(Jap)* Bear plus base

Kunstler *(Ger)* Skilled artisan, learned man

Kusaki *(Jap)* Grass plus tree

Lahti *(Fin)* Dweller near the bay

Langley, Langlois *(Fr)* The Englishman

Lanier *(Fr)* One who worked with wool

Lapidus *(Fr)* One who dealt in precious stones

Lapin *(Fr, Rus)* One who hunted, raised, or sold rabbits; one who had big feet

Le *(Chi)* Pear tree

Lederer *(Eng, Ger)* One who drove a vehicle, a carter

Ledermann *(Ger)* Leather maker, tanner

Lehrer *(Ger)* Teacher

Lejeune *(Fr)* The young man

Lesser *(Ger)* Custodian of a forest, gamekeeper

Levin, Levine *(Fr, Heb)* One who sold wine; dweller at the vine or vineyard; descendant of little Levi (united)

Li *(Chi, Kor)* Plums; black

Lichterman *(Ger)* One who lit lamps, a lamplighter

Lichtman *(Ger)* The light-complexioned man; one who made candles

Long *(Eng)* The tall one

Loughlin *(Scot)* One from the land of lochs (lakes)

Lowenthal *(Ger)* One who came from Lowenthal (lion valley) in Germany

Lumpp, Lump, Lumpe *(Eng)* Dweller at, or near, a deep pool or wooded valley; descendant of Lump, pet form of Lambert (land, bright)

Lustig *(Ger)* Happy

MacGowan *(Scot, Ir)* Son of the smith

Machado *(Sp, Port)* One who made and sold hatchets; one who used hatchets in his work

Macintosh *(Scot, Ir)* The son of chief or leader

Maldonado *(Sp)* Descendant of Donald (dark or brown-haired stranger)

Marinello *(It)* Dweller at the sign of the ladybug

Masada *(Jap)* Right plus rice field

Medina *(Sp)* Dweller at, or near, the market; one who had returned from Medina, the holy city of Islam; one who came from Medina, the name of several places in Spain

Meer *(Du, Ger)* One who dwells near a lake, or on the seacoast

Mehler, Mehlman, Melman *(Ger)* One who paints, a painter

Meltzer, Melzer *(Ger)* One who brews, a brewer; also one who came from Meltz, in Germany

Menaker *(Heb)* One who cleans the kosher meat

Menzies *(Scot)* One who came from Meyners, in Normandy

Metzger *(Ger)* Butcher

Miller *(Eng)* One who ground meal, grain, etc.

Mogilefsky *(Rus)* Dweller near a tomb or grave

Moneypenny *(Eng)* One with much money, a wealthy man; or ironically, a nickname for a poor man

Moody *(Eng)* The bold, impetuous, brave man

Mori *(Jap)* Forest

Morita *(Jap)* Forest plus rice field

Moshiah *(Heb)* Sephardic name, originally signified follower of Sabbatai Tzvi

Nachtman *(Ger)* One who worked as a night watchman

Nagano *(Jap)* Long plus field

Nagel *(Ger)* One who made nails

Nagy *(Hun)* The big man

Nakada *(Jap)* Middle plus rice field

Nakagawa *(Jap)* Middle plus river

Nakamura *(Jap)* Middle plus village

Nakashima *(Jap)* Middle plus island

Nakayama *(Jap)* Middle plus mountain

Nalbandian *(Arm)* The son of the man who shod horses

Ng *(Chi)* Crow; one who came from the province of Kiangsu

Nishi *(Jap)* West

Nishimura *(Jap)* West plus village

Novick, Nowicki *(Cz-Sl, Pol)* One who recently arrived in the area, a newcomer

Oh *(Chi)* Recklessly

Ono *(Jap)* Little plus field

Ostrow *(Pol)* Dweller on a small island in a river

Ota *(Jap)* Thick plus rice field

Ozawa *(Jap)* Little plus swamp

Pafko *(Cz-Sl)* Son of Palko, Czech form of Paul (small)

Palmiero, Palmieri *(It)* One who carries the palm in religious processions; one who granted or sold indulgences

Paluch *(Pol)* One with an unusual finger

Pancake *(Eng)* One who made and sold pancakes

Paredes *(Sp)* Dweller near the walls

Peabody *(Eng)* Nickname for a showily dressed individual

Pereira *(Port)* One who came from Pereira (pear tree), in Portugal; dweller near a pear tree

Perlmuter *(Ger)* Dealer in mother of pearl; possibly a name taken by one whose mother was named Perl

Piazza *(It)* Dweller at or near the square

Picasso *(Sp, It)* One who uses a pick or pickax in his work; one with the characteristics of a magpie

Pinsky, Pinski, Pinkser *(Rus, Ukr, Pol)* One who came from Pinsk, in Byelorussia

Plumer, Plomer *(Eng)* A dealer in plumes or feathers; also a variant of Plummer, one who worked with, or dealt in, lead

Podgorny *(Pol, Rus)* Dweller at the foot of the mountain

Poe *(Eng)* Dweller at the sign of the peacock; a nickname given to a proud or gaudily dressed man

Poland, Polan, Polland *(Eng)* Dweller at the homestead on which there was a pool, or through which a stream flowed; one who made and sold the long, pointed shoes worn in the 14th century

Pollack *(Ger, Fr)* One who came from Poland

Polsky *(Pol)* One who came from Poland, probably one who acquired the name outside of Poland

Pomerantz, Pomerance, Pomeranz *(Fr)* One who sold oranges

Portnoy *(Rus)* One who made outer garments, a tailor

Postman, Postmann *(Ger)* One who came from Postau

Power, Powers *(Eng, Ir)* The poor man, a pauper; one who had taken a vow of poverty

Profeta *(It)* One who played the part of the Prophet in play or pageant

Profitt, Proffit *(Eng, Scot, Fr)* One who acted the part of the Prophet in medieval pageants; a wealthy man

Ptashkin *(Rus)* Dweller at the sign of the small bird; one who trapped and sold small birds

Puttkamer *(Ger)* One who cleaned rooms

Quaglia, Quagliani *(It)* Dweller at the sign of the quail

Quayle *(Mx)* Son of Paul

Rabe *(Ger, Fr)* Descendant of the rabbi or teacher; dweller at the sign of the crow

Rabin *(Fr)* Descendant of the rabbi or teacher

Rabinovich, Rabinowitz *(Rus)* Descendant of the rabbi or Jewish teacher

Rader *(Ger)* One who made wheels, a wheelwright; one who occupied the office of alderman; one who came from Raden (moor, reedy place), in Germany; one who thatched with reed

Raitt, Rait, Raite *(Scot)* One who came from Rait (fort), the name of several places in Scotland

Raja, Rajah *(Hin)* Title of an Indian king, prince, or chief

Ramsay, Ramsey *(Scot, Eng)* One who came from Ramsay (ram's isle) in Scotland; or from Ramsey (wild garlic island), the name of places in Essex and Huntingdonshire

Rao *(Hin)* A Hindi title; also Italian name

Raudsepp *(Est)* One who worked in iron, a smith

Rausch *(Ger)* The excitable or hurried man; dweller near rushes

Reiber *(Ger)* One who worked at the baths, giving patrons a rubdown

Reifsneider, Reifsnyder *(Ger)* One who made barrel hoops

Reigle, Reigel *(Ger)* Dweller at the sign of the heron

Reiser *(Ger)* One who left to go to war; one from Reiser, in Germany

Reiter *(Ger)* One who rode a horse, a cavalryman; one who cleared land for tilling

Resnick *(Pol, Rus, Ukr)* One who sold meat, a butcher; one who slaughtered animals for meat according to Jewish ritual

Richter *(Ger)* One who held the office of judge or magistrate

Riegel *(Ger)* Dweller at the town fence; descendant of Ricoald (rule, power)

Ritchie, Ritchey *(Scot, Eng)* Descendant of little Rich, a pet form of Richard (rule, hard)

Rizzo *(It)* One who had curly or wavy hair

Rockne *(Nor)* An ancient farm name said to be older than written history

Rockower *(Ger)* One who came from Rockow (lowland) in Germany

Rogalski *(Pol)* Dweller near the Rogalskie (place frequented by animals with horns), a lake in Poland

Rothbart *(Ger)* Red beard

Rovin, Rovine, Rovins, Rovinsky *(Rus, Pol)* Dweller at a canal or ditch

Rozier *(Fr)* Dweller near a rosebush

Ruder, Ruderman *(Ger)* Nickname for a sailor

Rudnick, Rudinicki, Rudnik *(Pol)* One who worked in a mine; dweller near a mine; one who came from Rudnik (red), the name of many places in Poland and the Ukraine

Rusk *(Swe, Dan)* The valiant, brave, active man

Russell *(Eng)* The little red-haired man

Rychlak *(Pol)* One who was always early or ahead of time

Rys *(Eng)* Dweller near rushes, or in the brushwood

Sadowski *(Pol)* Dweller at, or near, an orchard

Saks *(Heb)* Acronym for *zera kedoshim Spiro*, descendants of the martyrs of Speyer (Spiro), in Germany

Saltz, Saltzman, Saltzmann *(Ger)* One who processed and sold salt

Sammoka *(Heb)* The red-haired

Sandler *(Ger)* One who carts sand; one who repaired shoes, a cobbler

Sanford *(Eng)* One who came from Sandford (sandy ford), the name of several places in England

Sangster *(Eng)* One who sang in church; a member of the chorus

Sato *(Jap)* Help plus wisteria

Savage *(Eng, Ir)* Wild or fierce man; one who had rough manners

Sayers, Sayre, Sayres, Sayer *(Eng)* One who sold silk or serge; one who assayed or tested metals, or tasted food; descendant of Saer or Sayer

Schatz *(Ger)* Treasure; *(Heb)* acronym for *shaliah tzibur*, leader of prayers in synagogue

Schenker *(Ger)* One who kept a public house, a publican

Scherer *(Ger)* One who shaved another, a barber; one who caught moles

Schlesinger *(Ger)* One who came from Silesia, or one who came from Schleusingen, in Thuringia

Schmucker, Schmuckler, Schmukler *(Ger)* One who decorates, embellishes, or ornaments things

Schneider *(Ger)* Tailor

Schreiber *(Ger)* Secretary or scribe

Schreiner *(Ger)* Cabinetmaker

Schubert *(Ger)* One who made and sold shoes

Schulman *(Ger)* School or synagogue man

Schuster *(Ger)* Shoemaker, cobbler

Schweizer, Schweitzer *(Ger)* One who came from Switzerland

Scott *(Eng)* One who came from Scotland; originally the word also included the Irish, one who came from Ireland

Selznick *(Ukr)* One who was thought to resemble a drake or a dragon

Seto *(Jap)* Rapids plus door

Shain, Shaine, Shaines *(Ger)* Beautiful or handsome person

Shanahan *(Ir)* Grandson of little Seanach (old, wise)

Shane *(Ir)* Descendant of Eion or Seon, Irish forms of John

Shapiro, Shapira, Shapero, Shapera *(Ger)* One from Speyer, in the middle ages spelled Spira, and by Jews spelled Shapira, in Bavaria

Shevchuk, Shevchenko *(Ukr)* The son of the shoemaker

Shimada *(Jap)* Island plus rice field

Shimizu *(Jap)* Pure plus water

Shirley *(Eng)* One who came from Shirley (wood belonging to the shire), the name of several places in England

Shoemaker *(Eng)* One who made and sold shoes and boots

Silberg *(Ger)* One from Silberg, the name of two places in Germany

Simonetti *(It)* Descendant of little Simon

Simson *(Eng)* Descendant of Sim or Simon

Sinclair *(Scot, Eng)* One who came from St. Clair, the name of several places in Normandy; a follower of St. Clare

Skelton *(Eng)* One who came from Skelton (the hill, or bank, manor), the name of parishes in Yorkshire and Cumberland

Skolnik, Skolnick *(Cz-Sl, Ukr)* The student, or one connected in some way with a school; an important functionary of the synagogue in the early Jewish communities

Skowron, Skowronski *(Pol)* Dweller at the sign of the lark; one who trapped larks

Skulsky *(Ukr, Rus)* One with a prominent cheekbone

Sleeper *(Eng)* One who made scabbards for swords; one who polished or sharpened swords

Sloan, Sloane *(Ir)* Grandson of Sluaghan (soldier, warrior)

Slocum *(Eng)* Dweller in a valley of blackthorn and sloe trees

Smethhurst *(Eng)* Dweller at the wood on smooth or level land; variant on smithhurst

Smith *(Eng)* Worker in metals

Sobel, Soble, Sobol, Sobelman *(Pol, Rus)* Dweller at the sign of the sable; one who trapped and sold sables

Song *(Chi)* To dwell (a dynasty name)

Spector, Specter, Spekter *(Rus)* A title meaning "inspector," used by Hebrew teachers in old Russia, which, when registered with the police, enabled them to live in areas forbidden to Jews

Speier *(Eng)* One who acted as a spy or watchman

Spitalny *(Pol)* Worker in a hospital (or dweller near one)

Spivak *(Pol, Ukr, Cz-Sl)* Cantor, one who sang in church or synagogue, especially a solo singer

Springfield *(Eng)* One who came from Springfield (spring or stream in open country), in Essex

Stamm *(Ger)* Dweller near an unusual tree trunk

Stanley *(Eng)* One who came from Stanley (stony meadow), the name of several places in England; dweller at a rocky meadow

Stastny *(Cz)* The happy, lucky, joyful man

Steadman *(Eng)* Dweller on a farmstead, a farm worker; one responsible for the care of warhorses

Stein *(Ger)* Dweller near a stone or rock, often a boundary mark; one who came from Stein, the name of numerous villages in Germany and Switzerland; descendant of Staino; a dweller in, or near, a stone castle

Steinhauer *(Ger)* One who cuts and builds with stone

Stengel *(Ger)* Dweller near a small pole

or stake

Stern, Sterne *(Eng, Ger)* The severe, austere man; dweller at the sign of the star, the star alluding to the Star of David

Sternberg *(Ger)* One who came from Sternberg (star mountain), the name of ten places in Germany

Stock *(Eng, Ger)* Dweller near a tree stump; dweller near a foot bridge

Storr *(Eng)* The big man; the strong, powerful man

Stroh *(Ger)* One who sold thatch for roofs

Studebaker *(Ger)* One who prepared or sold pastries

Sullivan *(Ir)* Grandson of Suileabhan (black-eyed)

Sussman, Susman *(Ger)* Sweet man, an affectionate person

Sutherland, Sutherlan, Sutherlin *(Eng)* One who came from the county of Sutherland (southern land) in Scotland

Sutter *(Eng)* One who made shoes, a shoemaker

Suzuki *(Jap)* Bell plus tree

Svoboda *(Cz-Sl, Pol, Ukr)* Liberty or freedom, a name suggesting a freeman, not a serf

Sweeney, Sweeny *(Ir, Eng)* Descendant of Suibhne (little hero); dweller on the island where pigs were kept; descendant of a peaceful or quiet man

Szabo *(Hun)* One who made outer garments, a tailor

Szasz *(Hun)* One who came from Saxony, a Saxon

Tabak, Taback, Tabachnick *(Pol)* One who prepared and sold snuff

Tagliaferro *(It)* One who cut or otherwise worked with iron

Tailleur *(Fr)* One who worked with outer garments, a tailor

Taylor, Tayler, Taylour *(Eng)* One who made outer garments, a tailor

Teitelbaum *(Ger)* The date palm tree, a name selected from Psalms 92:12: "The righteous shall flourish like the palm tree"

Teller *(Eng)* One who made or sold linen cloth

Ten Broeck *(Du)* Dweller at or near the marsh

Ten Eyck *(Du)* One who lived near an oak tree

Teng *(Chi)* Mound

Tenuto, Tenuta *(It)* Beloved, dear person

Tepper *(Eng)* One who furnished articles, especially arrows, with metal tips

Thatcher *(Eng)* One who covered roofs with straw, rushes, or reeds

Thayer *(Eng)* Descendant of Thaider (people, army)

Toomey, Tomey *(Ir)* Grandson of Tuaim (a sound)

Torme, Tormey *(Ir)* Grandson of Tormaigh (increase) or Thormodr

Treadwell *(Eng)* Dweller at a path, or road, by a stream or spring

Truman *(Eng)* The loyal servant

Tschudi *(Swi)* One who sat in judgment, a judge

Tsuji *(Jap)* Crossroads

Tuchman *(Ger)* One who deals in cloth

Tucker *(Eng)* One who cleaned and thickened cloth

Tung *(Chi)* To correct

Turner *(Eng)* One who fashioned objects on a lathe

Tuttle *(Eng)* Dweller at a toot-hill, that is a hill with a good outlook to detect an enemy's approach; also one who came from Tothill (lookout hill), the name of places in Lincolnshire and Middlesex

Tyler *(Eng)* One who made, sold, or covered buildings with tiles

Unruh *(Ger)* An agitator or troublemaker; one who was careless, restless, or indolent; one who came from Unruh in Germany

Updike, Updyck *(Du)* Dweller on the dike

Uyeda *(Jap)* Plant plus rice field

Uyeno *(Jap)* Upper plus field

Vaccaro, Vaccari, Vaccarello *(It)* One who tended cows

Voorsanger *(Du)* Cantor, singer

Wagner *(Ger)* Wagoner

Weber *(Ger)* Weaver

Wechsler *(Ger)* Money changer

Wright *(Eng)* One who worked in wood or other hard material; a carpenter

Yamashita *(Jap)* Mountain plus below

Youngman *(Eng, Ger)* The young servant

Pedigree Chart

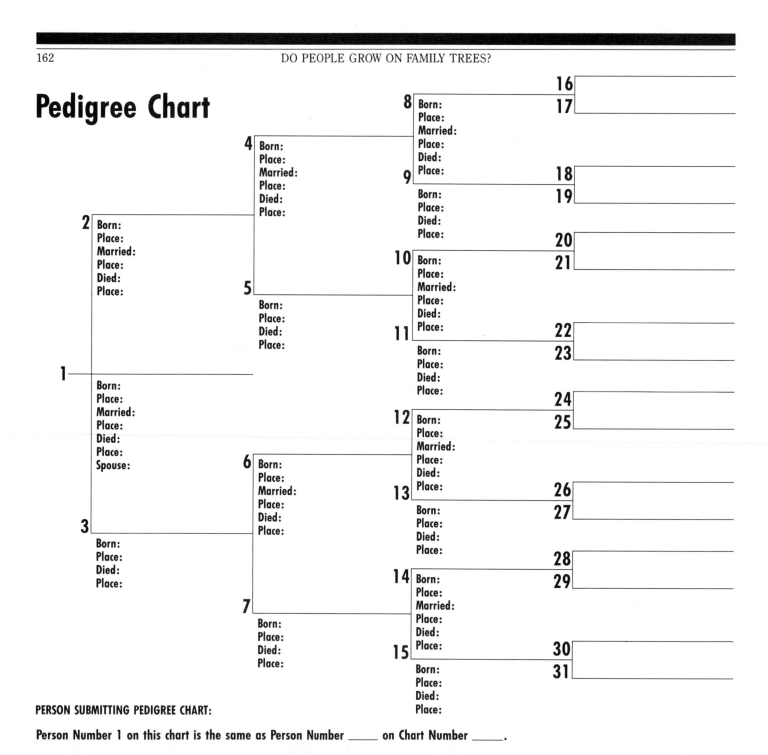

2 Born:
Place:
Married:
Place:
Died:
Place:

4 Born:
Place:
Married:
Place:
Died:
Place:

5 Born:
Place:
Died:
Place:

8 Born:
Place:
Married:
Place:
Died:
Place:

9 Born:
Place:
Died:
Place:

10 Born:
Place:
Married:
Place:
Died:
Place:

11 Born:
Place:
Died:
Place:

16

17

18

19

20

21

22

23

1

Born:
Place:
Married:
Place:
Died:
Place:
Spouse:

3 Born:
Place:
Died:
Place:

6 Born:
Place:
Married:
Place:
Died:
Place:

7 Born:
Place:
Died:
Place:

12 Born:
Place:
Married:
Place:
Died:
Place:

13 Born:
Place:
Died:
Place:

14 Born:
Place:
Married:
Place:
Died:
Place:

15 Born:
Place:
Died:
Place:

24

25

26

27

28

29

30

31

PERSON SUBMITTING PEDIGREE CHART:

Person Number 1 on this chart is the same as Person Number _____ on Chart Number _____.

Family Group Sheet

HUSBAND		WIFE	
Born	Place	**Born**	Place
Married	Place	——	
Died	Place	**Died**	Place
Buried	Place	**Buried**	Place
Husband's Father		Wife's Father	
Husband's Mother		Wife's Mother	
Husband's Other Wives		Wife's Other Husbands	

CHILDREN Last Name, First Name, Middle Name, Nickname or Other	WHEN BORN Day/Month/Year	WHERE BORN Town/County/State	DATE OF FIRST MARRIAGE To Whom	WHEN DIED Day/Month/Year

Sources of Information

Correspondence Log

Family Name _____

Date	Wrote to	Address	Subject	Reply

Abstract of Citizenship Papers
(Declaration of Intention, Petition)

My name _____   Today's date _____

Type of document _____   Where I found the document _____

Court where document was filed _____   Volume # _____   Page or petition # _____   Date filed _____

Applicant's name _____   Address _____

Name of ship to America _____

Where it left from _____   When _____   Where it arrived _____   When _____

Marriage information:
Name of spouse _____   Birthdate _____   Birthplace _____

Date of marriage _____   Place _____

Children:
Name _____   Birthdate _____   Birthplace _____

Name _____   Birthdate _____   Birthplace _____

Name _____   Birthdate _____   Birthplace _____

Witnesses listed on document:
Name _____   Address _____

Name _____   Address _____

Physical description of applicant:
Height _____   Weight _____   Race _____   Complexion _____

Eye color _____   Hair color _____   Occupation _____

Other documents I found _____

_____

Notes _____

1. Type of Request:
□ Freedom of Information Act (FOIA)   □ Privacy Act (PA)

2. Type or print below, the name, address and telephone number of the person to whom the information should be returned.

Name	Telephone number (Area code) ( )
Address (Street number and name)	(Apartment number)
(City)	(State)	(ZIP Code)

3. Action Requested:
□ Amendment (Privacy Act only)   □ Copy   □ Personal Review

4. Information needed to search for record(s):

Specific information, document(s), or record(s) desired.

Purpose for which desired. (You are not required to state the purpose for your request. Doing so *may* assist the INS in responding.)

5. Data for Identification of Personal Record (*Records normally cannot be located unless provided.)

*Family Name	Given Name	Middle Name
*Other Names used, if any	*Name used at time of entry into United States	
*Alien Registration number	*Place of birth	*Date of birth
Port abroad from which left for United States	Port of entry into United States	Date of entry
Manner of entry (air, sea, land, etc.)	Name of carrier (airline or vessel if applicable)	
*Name on Naturalization Certificate	Certificate number	Naturalization date
Address at time of Naturalization		
Naturalization Court and location		

6. Verification of identity:
□ In person with ID   □ Notarized Affidavit of identity   □ Other (specify)

7. Authorization/Consent (Usually required if requesting records about another person.)
□ I consent to allowing the person named below to see my record
□ Authorization letter/G-28/Power of Attorney/Other (specify)

Name of person authorized to see record	Signature of person giving consent

8. Fees: I agree to pay all costs incurred for search, duplication and review of materials up to $25.00, when applicable.

Signature of requester	Date	Telephone number (Area code) ( )

Form G-639 (Rev. 01/29/88) N

GENERAL INFORMATION

Please read all instructions carefully before completing this form. *Applicants making false statements are subject to criminal penalties [P.L. 93-579.88 stat. 1902 (5 U.S.C. 522a (i) (3))].*

The *Freedom of Information Act* (5 U.S.C. 552) allows requesters to have access to Federal agency records, except those which have been exempted by the Act.

The *Privacy Act of 1974* (5 U.S.C. 552a), with certain exceptions, permits individuals (United States citizens or permanent resident aliens) to gain access to information pertaining to themselves in Federal agency records, to have a copy made of all or any part thereof, to correct or amend such records, and to permit individuals to determine what records pertaining to themselves are collected, maintained, used, or disseminated. The Act also prohibits disclosure of individuals records without their written consent, except under certain circumstances.

INSTRUCTIONS

How to Submit a Request.
Persons requesting a search of INS records under the Feedom of Information or Privacy Acts may submit the completed application to the INS office nearest the applicant's place of residence. Requests may be submitted in person or by mail. If an application is mailed, the envelope should be clearly marked *"Freedom of Information"* or *"Privacy Act Information Request."*

Information Needed to Search for Records.
Failure to identify complete and specific information desired may result in a delay in processing or inability to locate the records or information requested.

Data for Identification of a Personal Record.
Complete as much of this section as possible; otherwise, there may not be enough information to locate the record(s) you want. Normally, records cannot be located without the person's name, date of birth, and place of birth, or the person's alien registration number or naturalization certificate number. Social Security Account Number (SSAN) is required for identification of Federal Government employee records.

Verification of Identity in Person.
An individual appearing in person may identify himself by showing a document bearing a photograph (such as an Alien Registration Card, Form I-151 or I-551, Citizen Identification Card, Form I-197, Naturalization Certificate, or passport); or two items which bear his name and address (such as driver's license and credit cards).

Verification of Identity by Mail.
An individual shall identify himself by full name, current address, date and place of birth and alien or employee identification number. A notarized example of his signature must also be provided. DOJ Form 361, Certification of Identity, may be used for this purpose.

Verification of Identity of Guardians.
Parents or legal guardians must establish their own identity as parents or legal guardians and the identity of the child or other person being represented.

Authorization or Consent.
Other parties requesting non-public information about an individual usually must have the consent of that individual on Form G-639 or by authorizing letter, together with appropriate verification of identity of the record subject.

Fees.
Except for commercial requesters, the first 100 pages of reproduction and two hours of search time will be furnished without charge. There is a fee of $.10 per page for photocopy duplication. For requests processed under the Freedom of Information Act, there may be a fee for quarter hours of time spent for searches for and review of records. Search fees are at the following rates: $2.25 clerical; $4.50 professional/computer operator; and $7.50 managerial. Other costs for searches and duplication will be charged at the actual direct cost. Fees will only be charged if the aggregate amount of search, copy, and/or review fees is more than $8.00. If the total anticipated fees amount to more than $250.00, an advance deposit of all of the fee may be required. Fee waivers or reductions may be *requested* for a request that clearly will benefit the public and is not primarily in the personal or commercial interest of the requester.

Manner of Submission of Fees When Required.
Do not send cash. Fees must be submitted in the exact amount. When requested to do so, submit a check or a United States Postal money order (or, if application is submitted from outside the United States, remittance may be made by bank international money order or foreign draft drawn on a financial institution in the United States) made payable to the "Immigration and Naturalization Service," in United States currency. An applicant residing in the U.S. Virgin Islands shall make his remittance payable to "Commissioner of Finance of the Virgin Islands," and, if residing in Guam, to "Treasurer, Guam."

A charge of $5.00 will be imposed if a check in payment of a fee is not honored by the bank on which it is drawn. Every remittance will be accepted subject to collection.

Privacy Act Statement.
Authority to collect this information is contained in Title 5, U.S.C. 552 and 552a. The purpose of the collection is to enable INS to locate applicable records and to respond to requests made under the Freedom of Information and Privacy Acts.

Routine Uses.
Information will be used to comply with requests for information under the Acts; maintain statistical data required under the Acts; and answer subsequent inquires concerning specific requests.

Effect of Not Providing Requested Information.
Furnishing the information requested on this form is voluntary. However, failure to furnish the information may result in the inability of INS to comply with a request, or refusal to comply with a request when compliance will violate other policies or laws.

Where to Write for Birth and Death Records

The best place to begin your document search is with vital records, especially birth, death, and marriage certificates. The list below, taken from the 1990 edition of "Where to Write for Vital Records," U.S. Department of Health and Human Services Publication No. (PHS) 90–1142, should help you locate birth and death records in any of the 50 states, Washington, D.C., and Puerto Rico. When you write, give as much information as possible about the event you are researching, and include a self-addressed, stamped envelope.

Alabama

Center for Health Statistics
State Department of Public Health
434 Monroe Street
Montgomery, AL 36130–1701

Alaska

Department of Health and Social
  Services
Bureau of Vital Statistics
P.O. Box H-02G
Juneau, AK 99811–0675

Arizona

Vital Records Section
Arizona Department of Health Services
P.O. Box 3887
Phoenix, AZ 85030

Arkansas

Division of Vital Records
Arkansas Department of Health
4815 West Markham Street
Little Rock, AR 72201

California

Vital Statistics Section
Department of Health Services
410 N Street
Sacramento, CA 95814

Colorado

Vital Records Section
Colorado Department of Health
4210 East 11th Avenue
Denver, CO 80220

Connecticut

Vital Records
Department of Health Services
150 Washington Street
Hartford, CT 06106

Delaware

Office of Vital Statistics
Division of Public Health
P.O. Box 637
Dover, DE 19903

District of Columbia

Vital Records Branch
Room 3009
425 I Street, NW
Washington, DC 20001

Florida

Department of Health and Rehabilitative
  Services
Office of Vital Statistics
1217 Pearl Street
Jacksonville, FL 32202

Georgia

Georgia Department of Human
  Resources
Vital Records Unit
Room 217-H
47 Trinity Avenue, SW
Atlanta, GA 30334

Hawaii

Office of Health Status Monitoring
State Department of Health
P.O. Box 3378
Honolulu, HI 96801

Idaho

Vital Statistics Unit
Idaho Department of Health and Welfare
450 West State Street
Statehouse Mail
Boise, ID 83720–9990

Illinois

Division of Vital Records
Illinois Department of Public Health
605 West Jefferson Street
Springfield, IL 62702–5079

Indiana

Vital Records Section
State Board of Health
1330 West Michigan Street
P.O. Box 1964
Indianapolis, IN 46206–1964

Iowa

Iowa Department of Public Health
Vital Records Section
Lucas Office Building
321 East 12th Street
Des Moines, IA 50319

Kansas

Office of Vital Statistics
Kansas State Department of Health and
   Environment
900 Jackson Street
Topeka, KS 66612–1290

Kentucky

Office of Vital Statistics
Department for Health Services
275 East Main Street
Frankfort, KY 40621

Louisiana

Vital Records Registry
Office of Public Health
325 Loyola Avenue
New Orleans, LA 70112

Maine

Office of Vital Records
Human Services Building
Station 11

State House
Augusta, ME 04333

Maryland

Division of Vital Records
Department of Health and Mental
   Hygiene
Metro Executive Building
4201 Patterson Avenue
P.O. Box 68760
Baltimore, MD 21215–0020

Massachusetts

Registry of Vital Records and Statistics
150 Tremont Street, Room B-3
Boston, MA 02111

Michigan

Office of the State Registrar and Center
   for Health Statistics
Michigan Department of Public Health
3423 North Logan Street
Lansing, MI 48909

Minnesota

Minnesota Department of Health
Section of Vital Statistics
717 Delaware Street, SE
P.O. Box 9441
Minneapolis, MN 55440

Mississippi

Vital Records
State Department of Health
2423 North State Street
Jackson, MS 39216

Missouri

Department of Health
Bureau of Vital Records
1730 East Elm
P.O. Box 570
Jefferson City, MO 65102

Montana

Bureau of Records and Statistics
State Department of Health and
   Environmental Sciences
Helena, MT 59620

Nebraska

Bureau of Vital Statistics
State Department of Health
301 Centennial Mall South
P.O. Box 95007
Lincoln, NE 68509–5007

Nevada

Division of Health-Vital Statistics
Capitol Complex
505 East King Street #102
Carson City, NV 89710

New Hampshire

Bureau of Vital Records
Health and Human Services Building
6 Hazen Drive
Concord, NH 03301

New Jersey

State Department of Health
Bureau of Vital Statistics CN 370
South Warren and Market Streets
Trenton, NJ 08625

New Mexico

Vital Statistics
New Mexico Health Services Division
1190 St. Francis Drive
Santa Fe, NM 87503

New York

(except New York City)
Vital Records Section
State Department of Health
Empire State Plaza
Tower Building
Albany, NY 12237-0023

New York City

Bureau of Vital Records
Department of Health of New York City
125 Worth Street
New York, NY 10013

North Carolina

Department of Environment, Health,
    and Natural Resources
Division of Epidemiology
Vital Records Section
225 North McDowell Street
P.O. Box 27687
Raleigh, NC 27611-7687

North Dakota

Division of Vital Records
State Capitol
600 East Boulevard Avenue
Bismarck, ND 58505

Ohio

Division of Vital Statistics

Ohio Department of Health
G-20 Ohio Department Building
65 South Front Street
Columbus, OH 43266-0333

Oklahoma

Vital Records Section
State Department of Health
1000 Northeast 10th Street
P.O. Box 53551
Oklahoma City, OK 73152

Oregon

Oregon Health Division
Vital Statistics Section
P.O. Box 116
Portland, OR 97207

Pennsylvania

Division of Vital Records
State Department of Health
Central Building
101 South Mercer Street
P.O. Box 1528
New Castle, PA 16103

Puerto Rico

Department of Health
Demographic Registry
P.O. Box 11854
Fernández Juncos Station
San Juan, PR 00910

Rhode Island

Division of Vital Records
Rhode Island Department of Health
Room 101, Cannon Building

3 Capitol Hill
Providence, RI 02908-5097

South Carolina

Office of Vital Records and Public Health
    Statistics
South Carolina Department of Health
    and Environmental Control
2600 Bull Street
Columbia, SC 29201

South Dakota

State Department of Health
Center for Health Policy and Statistics
Vital Records
523 E. Capitol
Pierre, SD 57501

Tennessee

Tennessee Vital Records
Department of Health and Environment
Cordell Hull Building
Nashville, TN 37219-5402

Texas

Bureau of Vital Statistics
Texas Department of Health
1100 West 49th Street
Austin, TX 78756-3191

Utah

Bureau of Vital Records
Utah Department of Health
288 North 1460 West
P.O. Box 16700
Salt Lake City, UT 84116-0700

Vermont

Vermont Department of Health
Vital Records Section
Box 70
60 Main Street
Burlington, VT 05402
(for records prior to 1955)
Division of Public Records
6 Baldwin Street
Montpelier, VT 05602

Virginia

Division of Vital Records
State Health Department
P.O. Box 1000
Richmond, VA 23208–1000

Washington

Vital Records
1112 South Quince
P.O. Box 9709, ET-11
Olympia, WA 98504–9709

West Virginia

Vital Registration Office
Division of Health
State Capitol Complex Bldg. 3
Charleston, WV 25305

Wisconsin

Vital Records
1 West Wilson Street
P.O. Box 309
Madison, WI 53701

Wyoming

Vital Records Services
Hathaway Building
Cheyenne, WY 82002

The National Archives Regional Archives System

If you are looking for an immigration or census document, the best place to start is the U.S. National Archives. This central clearing house for all federal government records has millions of documents on microfilm, including 130 years of ship arrival lists, 120 years of census records, and military and federal land-grant records.

The main branch of the National Archives is on the Mall in Washington, D.C. There are regional branch offices in many cities throughout the United States.

The following list gives you basic information about each branch of the archives. Be sure to call to verify that all information is still valid and to inquire about irregular evening and Saturday hours.

Main Branch

Eighth Street and Pennsylvania, NW,
   Washington, DC 20408
Hours: Monday to Friday, 8:45 AM to
   9:45 PM; Saturday, 8:45 AM to 5 PM
Phone: (202) 501-5402

New England Region

380 Trapelo Road, Waltham, MA 02154
States served: CT, MA, ME, NH, RI, VT
Hours: Monday to Friday, 8 AM to
   4:30 PM
Phone: 617-647-8100

Northeast Region

Building 22, MOT Bayonne, NJ 07002-
   5388
States served: NJ, NY, Puerto Rico, the
   Virgin Islands
Hours: Monday to Friday, 8 AM to
   4:30 PM
Phone: 201-823-7252

Mid-Atlantic Region

9th and Market Streets, Room 1350,
   Philadelphia, PA 19107
States served: DC, DE, MD, PA, VA, WV
Hours: Monday to Friday, 8 AM to 5 PM
Phone: 215-597-3000

Southeast Region

1557 St. Joseph Avenue, East Point, GA
   30344
States served: AL, FL, GA, KY, MS,
   NC, SC, TN
Hours: Monday to Friday, 7:30 AM to
   4:30 PM
Phone: 404-763-7477

Great Lakes Region

7358 South Pulaski Road, Chicago, IL
   60629
States served: IL, IN, MI, MN, OH, WI
Hours: Monday to Friday, 8 AM to
   4:30 PM
Phone: 312-581-7816

Central Plains Region

2312 East Bannister Road, Kansas City, MO 64131

States served: IA, KS, MO, NE

Hours: Monday to Friday, 8 AM to 4:30 PM

Phone: 816-926-6272

Southwest Region

501 West Felix Street (building address) P.O. Box 6216 (mailing address), Fort Worth, TX 76115

States served: AR, LA, NM, OK, TX

Hours: Monday to Friday, 8 AM to 4 PM

Phone: 817-334-5525

Rocky Mountain Region

Building 48, Denver Federal Center, Denver, CO 80225

States served: CO, MT, ND, SD, UT, WY

Hours: Monday to Friday, 7:30 AM to 3:45 PM

Phone: 303-236-0817

Pacific Southwest Region

24000 Avila Road, Laguna Niguel, CA 92677

States served: AZ, Southern California counties of Imperial, Inyo, Kern, Los Angeles, Orange, Riverside, San Bernadino, San Diego, San Luis Obispo, Santa Barbara, and Ventura; Nevada's Clark County

Hours: Monday to Friday, 8 AM to 4:30 PM

Phone: 714-643-4241

Pacific Sierra Region

1000 Commodore Drive, San Bruno, CA 94066

States served: CA (except southern counties covered under Los Angeles), HI, NV (except Clark County), and the Pacific Ocean area

Hours: Monday to Friday, 8 AM to 4:15 PM

Phone: 415-876-9009

Pacific Northwest Region

6125 Sand Point Way NE, Seattle, WA 98115

States served: ID, OR, WA

Hours: Monday to Friday, 7:45 AM to 4:15 PM

Phone: 206-526-6507

Alaska Region

654 West Third Avenue, Anchorage, AK 99501

States served: AK

Hours: Monday to Friday, 8 AM to 4 PM

Phone: 907-271-2441

Further Reading

I read through many sources while researching this book. Most of them would be useful to anyone who wants to do more exploring in the fascinating, never-ending field of genealogy.

About Immigration

Allen, Leslie. *Liberty: The Statue and the American Dream.* New York: Statue of Liberty/Ellis Island Foundation with National Geographic Society, 1985.

Antin, Mary. *The Promised Land.* Boston: Houghton Mifflin, 1912.

Archdeacon, Thomas J. *Becoming American: An Ethnic History.* New York: The Free Press, 1983.

Handlin, Oscar. *The Uprooted.* 2nd edition. Boston: Atlantic Monthly Press, 1973.

Heaps, Willard A. *The Story of Ellis Island.* New York: Seabury Press, 1967.

Kraut, Alan M. *The Huddled Masses: The Immigrant in American Society. 1880–1921.* Arlington Heights, Illinois: Harlan Davidson, Inc., 1982.

Morton Allan Directory of European Passenger Steamship Arrivals: For the years 1890 to 1930 at the Port of New York and for the years 1904 to 1926 at the Ports of New York, Philadelphia, Boston, and Baltimore. Baltimore: Genealogical Publishing Co., 1979.

Novotny, Ann. *Strangers at the Door: Ellis Island, Castle Garden, and the Great Migration to America*. Old Greenwich, Connecticut: Chatam Press, 1991.

Shapiro, Mary J. *Gateway to Liberty: The Story of the Statue of Liberty and Ellis Island*. New York: Vintage Books, 1986.

Stern, Gail F., editor. *Freedom's Doors: Immigrant Ports of Entry to the United States*. Catalog to exhibit published by the Balch Institute, Philadelphia, 1986.

Wheeler, Thomas, editor. *The Immigrant Experience: The Anguish of Becoming American*. New York: Dial Press, 1971.

Beginning Genealogy

Beller, Susan Provost. *Roots for Kids: A Genealogy Guide for Young People*. White Hall, Virginia: Betterway Publications, 1989.

Boyer, Carl III. *How to Publish and Market Your Family History*. 2nd edition. Newhall, California: Carl Boyer III Publisher, 1982.

Cosgriff, John and Carolyn. *Climb It Right: A High-Tech Genealogy Primer*. 2nd edition revised. Radford, Virginia: Heritage Press, 1986.

Crandall, Ralph. *Shaking Your Family Tree: A Basic Guide to Tracing Your*

Family's Genealogy. Dublin, New Hampshire: Yankee Publishing, 1986.

Croom, Emily Anne. *Unpuzzling Your Past: A Basic Guide to Genealogy*. 2nd edition. White Hall, Virginia: Betterway Publications, 1989.

Hilton, Suzanne. *Who Do You Think You Are?: Digging for Your Family Roots*. Philadelphia: Westminster Press, 1976.

Kyvig, David E., and Marty, Myron A. *Nearby History: Exploring the Past Around You*. Nashville, Tennessee: American Association for State and Local History, 1982.

Lichtman, Allan. *Your Family History: How to Use Oral History, Family Archives, & Public Documents to Discover Your Heritage*. New York: Vintage Books, 1978.

Pellowski, Anne. *The Family Storytelling Handbook: How to Use Stories, Anecdotes, Rhymes, Handkerchiefs, Paper and Other Objects to Enrich Your Family Traditions*. New York: Macmillan Publishing Co., 1987.

Perl, Lila. *The Great Ancestor Hunt: The Fun of Finding Out Who You Are*. Boston: Houghton Mifflin, 1989.

Shoumatoff, Alex. *The Mountain of Names: A History of the Human Family*. New York: Simon & Schuster, 1985.

Stone, Elizabeth. *Black Sheep and Kissing Cousins: How Our Family Stories Shape Us*. New York: Times Books, 1988.

Weitzman, David. *My Backyard History Book*. Boston: Little, Brown, 1975.

Westin, Jeane Eddy. *Finding Your Roots: How Every American Can Trace His Ancestors—At Home and Abroad*. Los Angeles: J. P. Tarcher, Inc., 1977.

Williams, Ethel W. *Know Your Ancestors: A Guide to Genealogical Research*. Rutland, Vermont: Charles E. Tuttle, Co., 1965.

Zimmerman, William. *How to Tape Instant Oral Histories*. 4th Printing. New York: Guarionex Press, 1988.

Advanced Genealogy

Cerny, Johni, and Eakle, Arlene. *Ancestry's Guide to Research: Case Studies in American Genealogy*. Salt Lake City, Utah: Ancestry Publishing, 1985.

Eakle, Arlene, and Cerny, Johni. *The Source: A Guidebook of American Genealogy*. Salt Lake City, Utah: Ancestry Publishing, 1984.

Everton, George B., Sr., editor. *The Handy Book for Genealogists*. 7th edition. Logan, Utah: Everton Publishers, 1981.

Groene, Bertram H. *Tracing Your Civil War Ancestor*. Winston-Salem, North Carolina: J.F. Blair, 1973.

Guzik, Estelle M., editor. *Genealogical Resources in the New York Metropolitan Area*. New York: Jewish Genealogical Society, 1989.

Neagles, James C. and Lila Lee. *Locating Your Immigrant Ancestor: A Guide to Naturalization Records*. Logan, Utah: Everton Publishers, 1975.

Ethnic Groups

Baxter, Angus. *In Search of Your British and Irish Roots: A Complete Guide to Tracing Your English, Welsh, Scottish and Irish Ancestors*. Baltimore: Genealogical Publishing Co., 1986.

_____. *In Search of Your European Roots: A Complete Guide to Tracing Your Ancestors in Every Country in Europe*. Baltimore: Genealogical Publishing Co., 1985.

_____. *In Search of Your German Roots: A Complete Guide to Tracing Your Ancestors in the Germanic Areas of Europe*. Baltimore: Genealogical Publishing Co., 1987.

Blockson, Charles L., and Fry, Ron. *Black Genealogy*. New York: Prentice-Hall, 1977.

Cohen, Chester G. *Shtetl Finder Gazetteer: Jewish Communities in the 19th and Early 20th Centuries in the Pale of Settlement of Russia and Poland, and in Lithuania, Latvia, Galicia, and Bukovina, with Names of Residents*. Bowie, Maryland: Heritage Books, Inc., 1989.

Kurzweil, Arthur. *From Generation to Generation*. New York: Schocken, 1982.

_____. *My Generations: A Course in Jewish Family History*. New York: Behrman House, 1983.

Meltzer, Milton. *World of Our Fathers*. New York: Dell Publishing, 1976.

Redford, Dorothy Spruill, with D'Orso, Michael. *Somerset Homecoming*. New York: Doubleday, 1988.

Rose, James, and Eichholz, Alice, editors. *Black Genesis: An Annotated Bibliography for Black Genealogical Research*. Detroit: Gale Books, 1977.

Smith, Jessie Carney. *Ethnic Genealogy: A Research Guide*. Westport, Connecticut: Greenwood Press, 1983.

Streets, David H. *Slave Genealogy: A Research Guide with Case Studies*. Bowie, Maryland: Heritage Books, 1986.

Names

Hook, J.N. *The Book of Names: A Celebration of Mainly American Names, People, Places and Things*. New York: Franklin Watts, 1983.

_____. *Family Names: The Origins, Meanings, Mutations, and History of More than 2,800 American Names*. New York: Macmillan Publishing Co., 1982.

Kaganoff, Benzion. *A Dictionary of Jewish Names and Their History*. New York: Schocken Books, 1977.

Lambert, Eloise, and Pei, Mario. *Our Names: Where They Came From and What They Mean*. New York: Lothrop, Lee and Shepard Co., 1960.

Meltzer, Milton. *A Book About Names*. New York: Thomas Y. Crowell, 1984.

Pine, L.G. *The Story of Surnames*. Rutland, Vermont: Charles E. Tuttle Co., 1966.

Smith, Elsdon C. *American Surnames*. New York: Chilton Publishing, 1969.

_____. *The Book of Smith*. New York: Nellen Publishing, 1974.

_____. *New Dictionary of American Family Names*. New York: Harper and Row, 1973. Gramercy Publishing reprint, 1988.

Index

A

Abdul-Jabbar, Kareem, 113
Accuracy, 93, 119, 121, 128, 153
Addresses, master lists of, 148–49
Address logs, 41
Adoptees, 133, 136–37
Adoptees Liberty Movement Association (ALMA), 136–37
Adoption Reunion Registry, 137
African-Americans, 26–27, 31, 96, 113, 133, 134–35
Ali, Muhammad, 113
Americanization, 94–103
American Revolution, 19
Ancestors, number of, 12
Antin, Mary, 14–15, 17, 49, 51, 102
Anuta, Michael J., 142
Arab-Americans, 96
Argentina, 43
Armenia, 96
Ashe, Arthur, 135
Asia, 30, 47, 103, 113
Australia, 43

B

Baltimore, 46
Baraka, Amiri, 113
Bartholdi, Frédéric-Auguste, 58
Basques, 96
Bedloe's Island, 58
Beginning a genealogical search, 6, 32–41
Belgium, 19, 96
Bibles, family, 77–78
Bibliography of Ship Passenger Lists, 1583–1825, 141
Birth certificates, 115, 116, 119–20, 144, 168–69
Black Genealogy, 135

Black Genesis, 135
Blockson, Charles L., 135
Boards of Special Inquiry, 62, 72
Boston, 46
Brazil, 43
Bremen, Germany, 44
Burstein, Abraham, 45
Burton Collection, 145
Busch, Irma, 45

C

Calendars, 136
Cambodia, 30
Camcorders, 83
Canada, 25, 43, 47, 74, 75, 96
Caribbean, 25, 30, 47
Castle Garden (New York City), 52
Cemetery records, 115, 121–22
Census records, 115, 122–24, 134, 138, 144
Central America, 47, 75
Changs, 109
Charleston, S.C., 46
Charts. *See* Genealogical charts
Cherokee, 134
Chickasaw, 134
China, 16, 24, 96, 97, 103, 109, 113
Chinese Exclusion Act, 29
Chmielniker Sick and Benevolent Society, 101
Chocktaw, 134
Church of Jesus Christ of Latter-Day Saints (Mormons), 91, 134, 135–36, 144–45
Citizenship papers, 116, 124, 125
   abstracts of, 118, 165
Civil War, 25
Cleveland, 27
Clothing industry, 99
Columbus, Christopher, 19
Congress, 29, 30, 51, 55–56, 122
Correspondence logs, 164
Cousins, 40
Cree, 134
Cuba, 96
Czechs, 96

D

Dallas Public Library, 145
Dates, confusion about, 128
Daughters of the American Revolution, 145
Death certificates, 115, 119–20, 121, 131, 144, 168–69
Declaration of Independence, 19
Declarations of Intention, 124, 125
Deeds, 131–32
Depression, Great, 30
Detroit, 27, 47
Detroit Public Library, 145
Directories, 142
Documents, 81, 86, 114–39, 147–48
   African-Americans and, 133, 134–35
   alternative places to look for information in, 131
   cemetery records, 115, 121–22
   census records, 115, 122–24, 134, 138, 144
   citizenship papers, 116, 124, 125
   deeds and land records, 131–32
   going to records centers for, 133
   military records, 116, 127–31, 135
   Native Americans and, 133, 134
   old-time handwriting in, 130
   passenger ship lists, 1, 51, 116, 124–27, 141
   preserving, 133
   relatives as sources of, 119
   religious records, 115, 120–21, 144
   school records, 116, 131
   tips on searching for, 116–19
   vital records, 115, 116, 119–20, 121, 131, 144, 168–69
   wills, 116, 132–33, 144
Dominican Republic, 96

E

Eastern Europe, 25, 46, 48, 103, 135–36
Economic opportunity, 15–16, 19, 30

Photo Credits

Frontispiece: Brown Brothers.
How I Became an Ancestor Detector
P. 2: *(left)* National Archives; *(right)* Ira Wolfman. **P. 3:** Ira Wolfman.
Chapter 1: Where You Came From
P. 5: Augustus F. Sherman Collection, Ellis Island Immigration Museum. **P. 6:** *(top)* Ellis Island Immigration Museum; *(bottom)* Lewis W. Hine Collection, U.S. History, Local History and Genealogy Division, The New York Public Library. **P. 7:** Augustus F. Sherman Collection, Ellis Island Immigration Museum. **P. 8:** Victoria & Albert Museum. **P. 9:** *(left)* Doubleday; *(right)* Courtesy of Alex Haley. **P. 10:** Courtesy of Alex Haley. **P. 11:** Courtesy of Joan Lince. **P. 12:** Carl Glassman. **P. 13:** Courtesy of Joan Lince.
Chapter 2: How We Got Here
P. 15: UPI/Bettmann. **P. 16:** Library of Congress. **P. 17:** UPI/Bettmann. **P. 18:** The New-York Historical Society, New York City. **P. 19:** *(left)* Picture Collection, The New York Public Library; *(right)* Chicago & North Western Railway. **P. 21:** Post card collection of Miriam Weiner. **PP. 22 & 23:** New-York Historical Society, New York City. **P. 24:** Association of American Railroads, Washington, D.C. **P. 25:** Library of Congress. **P. 28:** Ellis Island Immigration Museum. **P. 30:** Historical Association of Southern Florida. **P. 31:** Florida State Archives.
Chapter 3: Finding Your Families
P. 33: Ellis Island Immigration Museum. **PP. 35 & 39:** Picture Collection, The New York Public Library. **P. 41:** Ira Wolfman.
Chapter 4: Coming to America
P. 43: Post card collection of Miriam Weiner.

P. 45: Brown Brothers. **P. 46:** AP/Wide World Photos. **P. 47:** UPI/Bettmann. **P. 48:** *(left)* Ellis Island Immigration Museum; *(right)* Picture Collection, The New York Public Library. **P. 49:** Library of Congress. **P. 50:** The Mariner's Museum, Newport News, Virginia. **P. 52:** The New-York Historical Society, New York City. **P. 53:** Ellis Island Immigration Museum. **PP. 54 & 55:** Library of Congress. **P. 56:** Brown Brothers. **P. 57:** Photo by Alice Austen, Staten Island Historical Society. **PP. 58 & 59:** Ellis Island Immigration Museum. **P. 61:** William Williams Collection, U.S. History, Local History and Genealogy Division, The New York Public Library. **P. 62:** Library of Congress. **P. 63:** Smithsonian Institution (photo #49764). **P. 65:** Augustus F. Sherman Collection, Ellis Island Immigration Museum. **P. 66:** *(top)* Ellis Island Immigration Museum; *(bottom left)* UPI/Bettmann; *(bottom middle)* Augustus F. Sherman Collection, Ellis Island Immigration Museum; *(bottom right)* William Williams Collection, U.S. History, Local History and Genealogy Division, The New York Public Library. **P. 67:** *(top)* William Williams Collection, U.S. History, Local History and Genealogy Division, The New York Public Library; *(bottom left)* The Bettmann Archive; *(bottom right)* Augustus F. Sherman Collection, Ellis Island Immigration Museum. **P. 68:** Brown Brothers. **P. 69:** Library of Congress. **P. 70:** *(left)* Nicholas Cerulli ©; *(right)* Viviane Moos, Photo Reporters. **P. 71:** *(top four and bottom right)* Andrew Unangst, Next Commercial Productions; *(bottom left)* Nicholas Cerulli ©. **P. 72:** Brown Brothers. **P. 73:** William Williams Collection, U.S. History, Local History and Genealogy Division, The New York Public Library. **P. 74:** UPI/ Bettmann. **P. 75:** AP/Wide World Photos.

Chapter 5: Exploring The Past
PP. 77 & 78: Picture Collection, The New York Public Library. **P. 79:** Ira Wolfman. **P. 80:** *(left)* Florida State Archives; *(right)* Minnesota Historical Society. **P. 81:** Metaform, Ellis

Island Immigration Museum. **P. 82:** Comstock. **P. 84:** Ira Wolfman. **P. 85:** Yivo Institute for Jewish Research, Inc. **PP. 86 & 87:** Courtesy of Rona Beame. **P. 88:** Post card colletion of Miriam Weiner. **P. 89:** Picture Collection, The New York Public Library. **P. 90:** Florida State Archives. **P. 92:** Comstock. **P. 93:** Ira Wolfman.

Chapter 6: Becoming an American
P. 95: Library of Congress. **P. 97:** Picture Collection, The New York Public Library. **P. 98:** Jacob A. Riis Collection, Museum of the City of New York. **PP. 99 & 100:** Lewis W. Hine Collection, U.S. History, Local History & Genealogy Division, The New York Public Library. **P. 101:** Kit Barry, Brattleboro, Vermont. **P. 102:** UPI/Bettmann.
Chapter 7: The Name Game
P. 105: The Bettmann Archive. **P. 107:** Lewis Hine, George Eastman House Collection. **P. 108:** The Bettmann Archive. **P. 111:** Picture Collection, The New York Public Library.
Chapter 8: The Paper Chase
P. 115: Ira Wolfman. **PP. 116 & 118:** Collection of Miriam Weiner. **P. 117 & 119:** Post card collection of Miriam Weiner. **P. 120:** Boy Scouts of America. **P. 121:** Collection of Miriam Weiner. **P. 122:** UPI/Bettmann. **PP. 123 & 126 & 127:** Collection of Miriam Weiner. **P. 129:** State Archives of Michigan (negative #05166). **P. 130:** Picture Collection, The New York Public Library. **P. 132:** Ellis Island Immigration Museum. **P. 134:** Montana Historical Society, Helena. **P. 135:** Florida State Archives. **P. 137:** Ira Wolfman.
Chapter 9: You Could Look It Up
P. 141: Library of Congress. **P. 143:** National Archives. **P. 144:** Jo Nordhausen, © 1985, American Library Association.
Chapter 10: Sharing the Wealth
P. 147: Minnesota Historical Society. **P. 148:** Ira Wolfman. **P. 149:** Ellen Fisher Turk. **P. 151:** Dith Pran, The New York Times. **P. 153:** Ira Wolfman.